The Israel-Hamas War

Hal Marcovitz

San Diego, CA

About the Author

Hal Marcovitz is a former newspaper reporter and columnist who has written more than two hundred books for young readers. He makes his home in Chalfont, Pennsylvania.

© 2025 ReferencePoint Press, Inc.
Printed in the United States

For more information, contact:
ReferencePoint Press, Inc.
PO Box 27779
San Diego, CA 92198
www.ReferencePointPress.com

ALL RIGHTS RESERVED.
No part of this work covered by the copyright hereon may be reproduced or used in any form or by any means—graphic, electronic, or mechanical, including photocopying, recording, taping, web distribution, or information storage retrieval systems—without the written permission of the publisher.

Picture Credits:
Cover: Jose HERNANDEZ Camera 51/Shutterstock (top); Anas-Mohammed/Shutterstock (bottom)
 4: Shutterstock
 5: Shutterstock
 7: ZUMA Press, Inc./Alamy Stock Photo
12: Maury Aaseng
14: Pictorial Press Ltd/Alamy Stock Photo
17: Puffin's Pictures/Alamy Stock Photo
21: Eddie Gerald/Alamy Stock Photo
23: Ilia Yefimovich/dpa/picture-alliance/Newscom
26: Associated Press
29: Enrique Shore/Alamy Stock Photo
32: IDF/Polaris/Newscom
35: CHINE NOUVELLE/SIPA/Newscom
39: Mohammed Talatene/dpa/picture-alliance/Newscom
43: Abaca Press/Habboub Ramez/Abaca/Sipa USA/Newscom
45: dpa picture alliance/Alamy Stock Photo
49: Associated Press
52: UPI/Alamy Stock Photo
54: APFootage/Alamy Stock Photo

LIBRARY OF CONGRESS CATALOGING-IN-PUBLICATION DATA

Names: Marcovitz, Hal, author.
Title: The Israel-Hamas War / by Hal Marcovitz.
Description: San Diego, CA : ReferencePoint Press, 2025. | Includes bibliographical references and index.
Identifiers: LCCN 2024012676 (print) | LCCN 2024012677 (ebook) | ISBN 9781678209568 (library binding) | ISBN 9781678209575 (ebook)
Subjects: LCSH: Israel-Hamas War, 2023---Juvenile literature. | October 7 Hamas Attack, 2023--Juvenile literature. | Ḥarakat al-Muqāwamah al-Islāmīyah--Juvenile literature. | Gaza Strip--History--Juvenile literature.
Classification: LCC DS119.771 .M37 2025 (print) | LCC DS119.771 (ebook) | DDC 946.9405/4--dc23/eng/20240321
LC record available at https://lccn.loc.gov/2024012676
LC ebook record available at https://lccn.loc.gov/2024012677

CONTENTS

**Important Events in the
Israel-Hamas War**   **4**

Introduction   **6**
A Long and Simmering Feud Turns Lethal

Chapter One   **10**
Seeds of the Conflict

Chapter Two   **19**
Hamas Attacks

Chapter Three   **28**
Israel Strikes Back

Chapter Four   **37**
The Humanitarian Crisis

Chapter Five   **47**
The World Responds

Source Notes   57
For Further Research   61
Index   63

IMPORTANT EVENTS IN THE ISRAEL-HAMAS WAR

October 7: Hamas gunmen storm communities in southern Israel, killing more than twelve hundred people and taking more than two hundred hostages back to Gaza. Israeli prime minister Benjamin Netanyahu declares a state of war between Israel and Hamas, unleashing a missile attack on Gaza City.

October 27: Israel launches a broad ground offensive in northern Gaza.

November 14: Thousands of supporters of Israel attend the March for Israel rally in Washington, DC.

2023

October 9: Israel cuts off all electricity, food, water, and fuel to Gaza.

November 24: An agreed-on pause in fighting leads to the release of 105 Israeli hostages and more than 200 Palestinians held in Israeli jails. Some humanitarian aid is also allowed into Gaza.

October 13: Israel's military orders civilians to evacuate northern Gaza; ground troops conduct initial raids into Hamas-held territory.

October 21: Israeli troops permit a limited number of aid trucks carrying food to enter Gaza.

December 1: The temporary pause in fighting ends; Israel initiates a new round of missile attacks on the Gaza Strip.

January 21: Beneath the city of Khan Younis in the Gaza Strip, the Israeli military discovers a tunnel in which Israeli hostages had been held.

March 2: The US Air Force begins airdropping thousands of meals into northern Gaza.

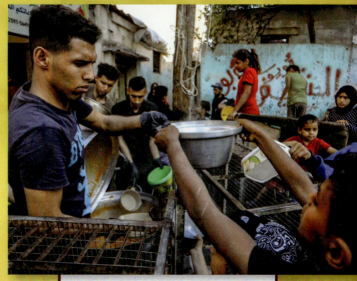

March 18: A UN-backed report says famine is imminent in northern Gaza and could spread to the rest of Gaza within months.

2024

February 29: The last hospital in northern Gaza closes, leaving thousands of Gazans without medical care.

March 4: A United Nations (UN) investigation reports that female victims of the October 7 Hamas attack were sexually assaulted before they were murdered.

March 3: Thousands of pro-Palestinian demonstrators attend a rally in New York City's Washington Square Park.

April 1: While delivering food to Gaza, seven workers for the international aid group World Central Kitchen are killed in an Israeli missile strike.

INTRODUCTION

A Long and Simmering Feud Turns Lethal

> "No fair-minded person could deny Israel the right of self-defense after the Hamas attack on Oct. 7 killed some 1,200 Israelis in one day. Women were sexually abused, and children were killed in front of their parents and parents in front of their children. Scores of abducted Israeli men, women, children and elderly people are still being held hostage in terrible conditions, now for more than 150 days.
>
> "But no fair-minded person can look at the Israeli campaign to destroy Hamas that has killed more than 30,000 Palestinians in Gaza, about a third of them fighters, and not conclude that something has gone terribly wrong there. The dead include thousands of children, and the survivors many orphans. So much of Gaza is now a wasteland of death and destruction, hunger and ruined homes."
>
> —Thomas L. Friedman, *New York Times* columnist
>
> Thomas L. Friedman, "Netanyahu Is Making Israel Radioactive," *New York Times*, March 12, 2024. www.nytimes.com.

It was just before 7:00 a.m. on October 7, 2023, when Sagui Dekel-Chen entered a small machine shop to begin his day's work on the grounds of Kibbutz Nir Oz. The kibbutz, with its 437 residents, is located in Israel about 1 mile (1.6 km) from the nation's border with the territory known as the Gaza Strip. Kibbutzim (plural for the Hebrew word *kibbutz*) were once mostly communal farms where dozens of residents lived and worked together. Today kibbutzim are more likely to be small, tightly-knit villages located far from the hustle and bustle of Israel's cities. About 2.8 percent of Israel's 9.3 million people live and work on one of the nation's approximately 270 kibbutzim.

> "Lock your doors and whoever has a weapon arm yourself."[1]
>
> —Sagui Dekel-Chen, a resident of Kibbutz Nir Oz

Within minutes of entering the machine shop, Dekel-Chen knew something was wrong. Glancing out a window, he saw armed men running through the kibbutz. Dekel-Chen made his way to the rooftop of the machine shop, where he could see numerous armed intruders. He quickly sent a text to all residents of Nir Oz: "I believe there are gunshots inside the kibbutz. Everybody: Lock your doors and whoever has a weapon arm yourself."[1]

Residents of kibbutzim in Israel have prepared for such attacks for decades. It is common for homes in kibbutzim to feature safe rooms—rooms in which residents can securely hide from attacks. The rooms can be locked from the inside and are buttressed with doors that cannot be forced open. After seeing the armed intruders, Dekel-Chen made his way to his home, locking his wife, Avital, and their two

Sagui Dekel-Chen had just started his workday in the Kibbutz Nir Oz machine shop when he realized the kibbutz was under attack. Dekel-Chen was abducted while defending the kibbutz. More than one hundred residents of the kibbutz were killed or taken hostage that day.

daughters in the safe room. Then the thirty-five-year-old father—who had emigrated from America at age eighteen—armed himself with a gun, made his way back to the streets of Nir Oz, and prepared to defend the kibbutz alongside his neighbors.

Attack on Gaza City

Within hours of the attack on Nir Oz, missiles launched from Israel started striking targets in Gaza City, a city of some eight hundred thousand residents in the Gaza Strip. Entire neighborhoods in Gaza City were wiped out by the missiles, and hundreds of civilians were killed. Eman Abu Saeid, a mother of two young children who lived in Gaza City, described the early hours of the Israeli attack:

> We woke up with the dust bombing on our faces and bodies and smelling of gunpowder and dirt. My kids crying and shouting all the day because of the bombing from the . . . war airplanes from the Israeli occupation. And we feel helpless, afraid. . . .
>
> Kids are dead, mothers dead. They are just full of dust. . . . Yes, it's a horrible, horrible, horrible thing to see here in Gaza. And I try to make my kids safe.[2]

Soon after the attack commenced, Abu Saeid and her family fled to another city in the Gaza Strip. But weeks later, an Israeli missile struck an apartment building where the family found shelter after leaving Gaza City. Abu Saeid, her husband, and the couple's two children were killed in the blast.

Relentless and Deadly

The missiles had been launched by Israel in response to the October 7 assault on Nir Oz and several other communities. The surprise attack on Israel had been carried out by Hamas, the militant Palestinian group that controls Gaza. That attack resulted in the deaths of some twelve hundred Israelis, many of whom were tortured, mutilated, or raped. In addition, Hamas kidnapped more than two hundred Israeli citizens and took them back to Gaza, where they were held hostage. Sagui Dekel-Chen was among the hostages taken that day, captured as he attempted to defend the Nir Oz kibbutz. More than 100 of Nir Oz's 437 residents were either killed or taken hostage by Hamas. "My daughter-in-law and the kids are now traumatized," said Sagui's father, Jonathan Dekel-Chen. "Avital heard her husband struggling in hand-to-hand combat."[3]

> "We woke up with the dust bombing on our faces and bodies and smelling of gunpowder and dirt. My kids crying and shouting all the day because of the bombing."[2]
>
> —Eman Abu Saeid, a resident of Gaza

The attack by Hamas sparked a relentless and deadly response by Israel that continued for months. Israel's military rained missiles down on the Gaza Strip while Israeli soldiers crossed over the border as they carried out their pursuit of Hamas militants. Israel's leaders vowed to wipe out Hamas—a mission that had resulted in the deaths of more than thirty thousand Gaza residents by the spring of 2024. Moreover, tens of thousands of Gazans were forced to flee their homes. Many of those homes were destroyed by Israeli missiles. In its effort to flush out the Hamas fighters, Israel had cut off access to Gaza's food, water, and electricity.

Israelis and Palestinians—two ethnic groups who claim the same land—have harbored feelings of suspicion, anger, and hatred toward one another for decades. Over the years, efforts to resolve the friction between these two groups have seen little progress. The October 7 attack by Hamas provoked Israel into responding with its formidable military, touching off a level of violence that shocked the world.

CHAPTER ONE

Seeds of the Conflict

> "One year matters more than any other for understanding the Israeli-Palestinian conflict. In 1948, Jews realized their wildly improbable dream of a state, and Palestinians experienced the mass flight and expulsion called the Nakba, or catastrophe. The events are burned into the collective memories of these two peoples—often in diametrically opposed ways—and continue to shape their trajectories."
>
> —Emily Bazelon, *New York Times Magazine* writer
>
> Emily Bazelon, "The Road to 1948," *New York Times Magazine*, February 1, 2024. www.nytimes.com.

To understand why the group Hamas launched the attack on Israel, and why Israel struck back with such fierce and deadly resolve, one has to look back at decades of distrust, suspicion, and tension that have existed between Israel and its neighbors in the Middle East. In the past, Arab states in the Middle East waged war against Israel with the goal of driving the Jewish nation out of the region. These efforts did not succeed. In subsequent years, some of these Arab states have made peace with Israel. Hamas has never done so. Its stated goal has always been the destruction of Israel. And although Israel has relations with some of its neighbors, its government has become increasingly strident when dealing with the Palestinian people.

The Founding of Israel

The nation of Israel was established in 1948, three years after the end of World War II—a time when European Jews were targeted for elimination by the Nazi regime that had taken power in Germany in 1933. The Jews were victims of what is known as the Holocaust—millions of Jews in European nations conquered by the Nazis were taken from their homes and imprisoned in concentration camps. When the war ended in 1945, some 6 million Jews had been murdered by the Nazis. The survivors were homeless. The United Nations (UN), formed in the aftermath of the war, established a homeland for the Jews in the Middle Eastern land that had been their ancestral home, off and on, for millennia.

Many survivors of the concentration camps made their way to the new nation of Israel. So did many Jews living in nearby Arab nations and other parts of the world. Over the next eight decades, the Israelis built a vibrant, modern, democratic nation. They also dedicated themselves to establishing a strong military to protect their citizens against the type of aggression that had been perpetrated by the Nazis. Service in the military—known as the Israel Defense Forces (IDF)—is mandatory for all Israeli young adults. Aided in no small measure by the United States and other allies, the IDF has at its disposal a significant arsenal of modern weapons and intelligence services.

The First War

For decades the territory where the nation of Israel would eventually be established had been known, unofficially, as Palestine. (The name finds its origins in the story of the Philistines: migrants from ancient Greece who settled in the region in the twelfth century BCE.) For centuries the region had been under the domain of the Ottoman Empire. Vast and powerful, the Ottoman Empire was Muslim, led by a royal family and based in what is now the nation of Turkey. But in 1914, at the outbreak of World War I, the Ottomans allied with the Germans in the conflict against the British, French, and, eventually, Americans. After the war the Ottoman Empire was broken up into individual nations. Palestine fell under the control of the British government and remained under a British mandate until Israel was established following World War II. Israel was carved out

Israel, Gaza, and West Bank

of territory along the Mediterranean Sea. The nation spans about 290 miles (467 km) north to south and about 85 miles (137 km) east to west at its widest point. It shares borders with Egypt, Jordan, Syria, and Lebanon.

Over the centuries many diverse peoples had made their home in Palestine, among them Christians, Muslims, and Jews. For centuries Muslims have made up a majority of the population of the region. The UN mandate that created Israel also set aside land for the Palestinian people—but the Palestinians, who had been living in what was now Israel, as well as the neighboring Arabic nations refused to accept the UN mandate. They believed that the Western powers behind the UN mandate—the Americans and British, among them—were exercising the same degree of colonialism that over the centuries had led to the domination by the Ottomans and then the British. Immediately after Israel's formation in 1948, the Palestinians and their allies in neighboring Arab countries attacked the new nation. The war lasted about a year, ending when the UN brokered a ceasefire.

Under the terms of the ceasefire, Israel's statehood was ensured, while two neighboring territories—Gaza and the West Bank—were placed under the administration of Arab nations. Gaza fell under the administration of Egypt, while Jordan oversaw the West Bank. According to the UN, these two regions were now home to about 570,000 Palestinians who either fled or were forced out during the war or shortly after the ceasefire was declared. The result was to further establish Israel as a state governed by a Jewish majority and to solidify for Palestinians the event they call the *Nakba*, or catastrophe. Within Gaza and the West Bank, a movement to create an independent Palestinian nation was born. Although there was no direct geographic connection between the two territories, as they lay several miles apart, they would be administered by a single Palestinian government. Gaza is a small strip of land, about 25 miles long (40 km) and no more than 8 miles (13 km) wide. About 53 miles (85 km) across Israel to the east lies the West Bank. The West Bank is about 80 miles (129 km) in length and about 35 miles (56 km) wide.

The Oslo Accord

Despite the ceasefire following the 1948 war, tensions remained high. In 1967 war erupted when several Arab nations attacked Israel. The war lasted a mere six days—it is known as the Six-Day War—resulting in a sweeping Israeli victory. Following the war, Israeli

The Birth of Zionism

In approving the establishment of Israel, the United Nations acted on a proposal that dated back to the late nineteenth century first made by activist Theodor Herzl, founder of a movement known as Zionism. For centuries, Jews had referred to a region in the Middle East bordering the Mediterranean Sea as Zion—the place where the first Israelite settlers established their homes some thirty-six hundred years ago.

Herzl's plan to establish a Jewish homeland was sparked by the 1894 trial of Alfred Dreyfus, a Jewish officer in the French army who had been unjustly accused of treason. A journalist, Herzl attended the Dreyfus trial and witnessed French mobs shouting "Death to the Jews." Herzl realized then that European Jews were not safe in their home countries—a fact confirmed years later by the murders of 6 million European Jews during World War II. It was Herzl who first proposed a mass exodus of Jews from Europe to a homeland in the Middle East. Says Itamar Rabinovich, a professor of history at Tel Aviv University in Israel, "The world felt that it owed the Jewish people after the Holocaust. The basic argument of Zionism—that the Jews are not safe—was vindicated by the deaths of six million."

Quoted in Emily Bazelon, "The Road to 1948," *New York Times Magazine*, February 1, 2024. www.nytimes.com.

forces occupied Gaza and the West Bank. Israel sent troops into the two territories to maintain security.

During this period hundreds of thousands of Palestinians left the two territories, becoming refugees in nearby Arab countries, among them Egypt and Jordan. Another war erupted in 1973. This time, the fighting lasted nearly a month, ending in a cease-fire that resulted in no change in the status of a proposed self-governing Palestinian homeland.

But diplomatic efforts to resolve the differences in the region commenced. In 1979 Israel signed a peace treaty with Egypt. In 1994 Jordan signed a similar treaty with Israel. In subsequent years the Arabic countries of Bahrain, Morocco, Sudan, and the United Arab Emirates signed treaties with Israel as well. However, Israel was still under threat of attack—chiefly by the Palestinian Liberation Organization (PLO), a militant group founded in 1964 with the aim of driving the Israelis out of the region. The PLO

US president Bill Clinton is flanked by Israeli prime minister Yitzhak Rabin (left) and PLO chairman Yasser Arafat (right) at the signing of the Oslo Accord in 1993. The agreement raised hopes for security and recognition for Israel and a state for the Palestinians.

The Failures of the Palestinian Authority

When the Likud political party ascended to power in Israel, its leaders refused to negotiate with the Palestinian Authority, the body established by the 1993 Oslo Accord to eventually become the government in Gaza and the West Bank. Under the Oslo Accord, the transition to a Palestinian nation under its own government was supposed to occur within five years—but it has yet to happen.

Over the years, the Palestinian Authority has shouldered criticism for its dysfunction. By 2024 the Palestinian Authority was under the leadership of eighty-eight-year-old Mahmoud Abbas, who at the time had been head of the organization for more than twenty years. During his years as president of the Palestinian Authority, Abbas was known to tolerate no dissent in the ranks. He often expelled officials who disagreed with his strategies for establishing a Palestinian state. He has even been accused of ordering the assassinations of rivals.

Some diplomats believe the Palestinian Authority should still eventually be recognized as the rightful government in Gaza and the West Bank, but for that to happen Abbas would have to be ousted as its leader. Said one diplomat, "A lot more will have to happen for real change, including at the top."

Quoted in Steve Hendrix and Loveday Morris, "Palestinian Leaders Resign, but Abbas Hangs Onto Power," February 29, 2024, *Philadelphia Inquirer*, p. A3.

and similar groups often resorted to terrorist tactics. At the 1972 Olympics in Munich, Germany, members of the Israeli Olympic team were taken hostage by a radical offshoot of the PLO. Five of the hostage takers were killed, as were eleven Israeli athletes and one West German police officer. And in 1976, terrorists hijacked an Air France flight from Israel to France while it was on a layover in Greece. The hijackers forced the plane to land in Uganda, where they separated approximately one hundred Jewish and Israeli passengers from the others and demanded the release of Muslims imprisoned in Israel and other countries. The standoff ended when the terrorists were killed by Israeli commandos who flew in to rescue the hostages. One Israeli soldier and three hostages also died. Both events served only to sharpen the animosity between the two sides.

After decades of such turmoil, though, hopes for a separate Palestinian state were bolstered in 1993 when leaders of the Israeli government and the PLO signed a treaty known as the Oslo Accord. According to the treaty, the PLO renounced terrorism and recognized Israel's right to exist. Israel agreed to cede authority over Gaza and the West Bank to an entity to be known as the Palestinian Authority, which would eventually administer an independent Palestinian nation. The goal of the Oslo Accord became known as the "two-state solution." In other words, there would be a single state, Israel, for the Jewish people, and a single state, Palestine, for the Palestinians.

The Oslo Accord held great promise, but after its approval, little happened to create an official Palestinian state. Many Israelis remained suspicious of the Palestinians. Years earlier, the conservative Likud Party had begun to attract support among Israeli voters. The party made no secret of its opposition to a Palestinian state. In 1983 the Likud Party gained control of a majority of seats in the Israeli parliament, and although in subsequent years it has lost its majority from time to time, for much of the past two decades the Likud Party has governed Israel—most of that time under the leadership of Prime Minister Benjamin Netanyahu.

The Likud Party Takes Over

Under the Likud Party–led Israeli government, Jewish settlements were established in Gaza and the West Bank. This meant that new communities consisting of Jewish residents were erected in territories that, under the Oslo Accord, were supposed to be granted complete autonomy from Israel. Many diplomats and others believed the Israeli government's settlement policy was an attempt to enlarge Israel's borders to include Gaza and the West Bank. The settlements were strongly opposed by the Palestinians. Acts of protest, often violent, were common. In 2005 Israel agreed to close down the settlements in Gaza, but Jewish settlements in the West Bank have continued. By 2024 there were more than two hundred such communities, comprising some seven hundred thousand Jewish residents. "What worries me the most is that these agreements [to establish West Bank settlements] change the democratic structure of what we know of as the state of Israel," says Tomer Naor, a leader of the Movement for Quality Government in Israel, an independent government watchdog group.

"One day we'll all wake up and Netanyahu is not going to be prime minister, but some of these changes will be irreversible."[4]

> "One day we'll all wake up and Netanyahu is not going to be prime minister, but some of these changes will be irreversible."[4]
>
> —Tomer Naor, a leader of the Movement for Quality Government in Israel

Over the years Netanyahu has made it clear he opposes a separate Palestinian state. As far back as 2015, he had this to say on the issue: "Whoever moves to establish a Palestinian state or intends to withdraw from [Israeli-held] territory is simply yielding territory for radical Islamic terrorist attacks against Israel."[5] Since ascending to power in Israel, the Likud Party and Netanyahu, as its leader, have refused to negotiate with the Palestinian Authority to create an independent Palestinian nation.

Within Gaza, militants grew frustrated with the inability of the Palestinian Authority to achieve statehood. Moreover, in the decades since Israel rose to be a powerful leader in the international economy, Gaza and the West Bank have remained mired in poverty. Both territories lack the industries that would enable their citizens to find employment and lead comfortable lives. A 2023 report by the international economic aid organization World Bank, released six months before the October 7 Hamas attack, found unemployment in Gaza at nearly 50 percent. In contrast, the unemployment rate reported in Israel in 2023 was a mere 3.5 percent.

In October 2023, shortly after the Hamas attack on Israel, a protester raises a sign inscribed with a popular slogan that calls for the obliteration of Israel.

A Call to Obliterate Israel

In 1987 the group known as Hamas was formed. *Hamas* is an acronym for the Arabic name Harakat al-Muqawama al-Islamiya (in English, the Islamic Resistance Movement.) Since its founding, Hamas has committed numerous terrorist acts against Israelis and in 1997 was designated a terrorist organization by the US Department of State. But within Gaza, Hamas's influence continued to grow, and since 2007 the group has served as the de facto government in Gaza, displacing the UN-created Palestinian Authority.

During that time, Hamas militants have been motivated not by the establishment of an independent Palestinian state beside an independent Israeli state, but rather by the desire to destroy Israel. Many Palestinian militants have rallied around the declaration "From the river to the sea, Palestine will be free"—meaning the region from the Jordan River to the Mediterranean Sea, the land occupied by Israel, would be swept free of its Jewish occupants and dedicated solely to a Palestinian state. Says Thomas L. Friedman, foreign affairs columnist for the *New York Times*, "Hamas has never wavered from being more interested in destroying the Jewish state than in building a Palestinian state—because that goal of annihilating Israel is what has enabled Hamas to justify its hold on power indefinitely, even though Gaza has known only economic misery since Hamas seized control."[6]

> "Hamas has never wavered from being more interested in destroying the Jewish state than in building a Palestinian state."[6]
>
> —Thomas L. Friedman, foreign affairs columnist for the *New York Times*

For decades, then, Israel and Gaza have shared a common border but have never come close to a peaceful resolution that would result in an independent Palestinian state in Gaza as well as in the West Bank—or recognition by Hamas that Israel has a right to exist. Finally, on October 7, 2023, Hamas sent militants across the border into Israel to take hostages and commit murder—believing this act would be the first step toward the annihilation of Israel. And Israel—a nation born in the wake of the tragic events of the Holocaust—responded not with diplomacy but with missile strikes.

CHAPTER TWO

Hamas Attacks

> "I hope that the state of war with Israel will become permanent on all the borders, and that the Arab world will stand with us."
>
> —Taher El-Nounou, a Hamas spokesperson
>
> Quoted in Ben Hubbard and Maria Abi-Habib, "Behind Hamas's Bloody Gambit to Create a 'Permanent' State of War," *New York Times*, November 8, 2023. www.nytimes.com.

For months, young people in Israel looked forward to Supernova—a music festival planned for October 6 and 7, 2023, marking the end of the Jewish holiday of Sukkot. The holiday is an annual weeklong celebration that commemorates the liberation of Hebrew slaves from ancient Egypt. Organizers of Supernova planned to stage the event in Israel's Negev Desert—about 3 miles (4.8 km) from the Gaza border. It is a sprawling, grassless area where Supernova's organizers erected tents, food stands, electronic music amplifiers, and stages for the DJs.

By the early morning hours of October 7, more than three thousand fans were in attendance. But at about six o'clock that morning, the pulsing beats generated by the DJs onstage were replaced by a much different sound: explosions. Says Michael Ohana, a twenty-seven-year-old Israeli who attended the festival, "We arrived at the party at 3 o'clock in the morning, all the friends met and celebrated life. At 6 a.m., the hell started."[7]

Rockets launched from only a few miles away in Gaza rained down on the festival grounds. Many attendees dropped to the ground to avoid getting hit by the shrapnel that burst from the rockets. Others ran through the festival grounds, looking for cover. Many attendees tried to escape the turmoil by running to their cars in the nearby parking area.

> "We arrived at the party at 3 o'clock in the morning, all the friends met and celebrated life. At 6 a.m., the hell started."[7]
>
> —Michael Ohana, an attendee at the Supernova music festival

Minutes later, dozens of armed Hamas militants entered the festival grounds and started firing into the crowd. The festival attendees who tried to drive away from the scene found the roads blocked by armed Hamas fighters. "People were panicking," says festival attendee Yoni Diller. "Suddenly, we see this car bumping into another car very slowly. The door opens, and we see a wounded girl. Someone shot her in the leg, and her whole left knee was disconnected from her body. She couldn't brake. Her knee was shot. We tried to help her [and] give her water. She was dying in front of our eyes."[8]

Over several hours, the Hamas militants murdered 364 festivalgoers, according to reports in the Israeli media. "There were these crazy maniacs with guns and people falling one by one," says Hila Fakliro, who attended the festival. "It was like a shooting range."[9] Another forty people were captured and taken back to Gaza to be held as hostages.

Rockets Rain Down on the Cities

The October 7 attack was not limited to the Supernova festival. At about 6:30 a.m., air raid sirens shattered the early morning calm in several Israeli cities, among them Tel Aviv, Rehovot, Gedera, and Ashkelon. Dozens of rockets rained down on those cities. In the city of Ashkelon, on the Mediterranean coast, a hospital was hit by a rocket. In other cities, homes and commercial properties were struck by the rockets.

Ari, a twenty-nine-year-old resident of Tel Aviv—Israel's largest city—said he awoke early in the morning of October 7 to the sound of air raid sirens. Because of the long history of animosity between Israel and its neighbors, underground bomb shelters have been built throughout Israel's cities and towns. Ari hurried to a bomb shelter directly behind his apartment building. "Behind my building on the main road, people were running into the bomb shelter," Ari says. "I was the last one in. There were kids streaming in and I was

An Israeli soldier places a rose near the photo of one of the 364 people killed by Hamas at the Supernova Music Festival on October 7. Photos of other murdered festivalgoers have been erected at the site.

throwing them down. Just before I got down, we heard a massive boom. I looked behind and there was smoke billowing out."[10]

In northern Israel, American Kalina Bitter was seated on a tour bus headed for the town of Nazareth when she heard the air raid sirens, warning of approaching missiles. "I didn't know how to take it," says Bitter, an officer in the US Navy. "Some of the people in our group were panicking, but we didn't really know the extent of what was happening." Bitter's tour group returned to their hotel in Jerusalem, where they found the usually bustling streets of the city empty. Jerusalem had also been targeted by Hamas rockets. "Things were kind of ominous and weird," she says. "All week long, there'd been thousands and thousands of people singing and dancing, celebrating the Jewish holiday Sukkot. You couldn't walk it was so packed. The difference as we neared the hotel was like night and day."[11]

> "Just before I got down, we heard a massive boom. I looked behind and there was smoke billowing out."[10]
>
> —Ari, a resident of Tel Aviv

How Did the Mossad Miss the Warning Signs?

Israel's intelligence agency is known as the Mossad (a Hebrew word that means "Institute.") Through the use of electronic surveillance as well as a network of spies and informants, the Mossad is charged with providing intelligence to the IDF on the activities of Israel's enemies. And yet the Mossad missed the warning signs indicating that Hamas was planning the October 7, 2023, attack.

Intelligence experts believe it is likely the Mossad—as well as US-based spy agencies—did develop intelligence on the impending attack but that the information was likely still being assessed by military leaders who were not yet convinced an attack was imminent. Says Emily Harding, a national security analyst at the Washington, DC–based Center for Strategic and International Studies:

> The intelligence community knew plotting was ongoing, but the warning was too general to result in decisive, preventive action or improved defenses. Policymakers often expect precision: an attack by this entity will occur at this place at this time. Rarely—if ever—does a picture that clear come together. The Hamas assault on Israel may turn into a case of nonspecific warning: some reports indicate that US and Israeli intelligence were watching for rising tensions, but there was no precise warning of an impending attack.

Emily Harding, "How Could Israeli Intelligence Miss the Hamas Invasion Plans?," Center for Strategic and International Studies, October 11, 2023. www.csis.org.

Attack on Be'eri

As rockets rained down on Israeli cities, Hamas militants continued to cross the border, shooting and kidnapping unarmed civilians. The Supernova festival was just one of their targets. Many of the kibbutzim located near the Gaza border, among them Nir Oz, were overrun with Hamas fighters.

Kibbutz Be'eri, located about 3 miles (4.8 km) from Gaza, was overrun by Hamas militants in the early morning hours of October 7. Shortly before seven o'clock that morning, kibbutz resident Gal Cohen was walking his dog when he saw two men riding motorbikes through the kibbutz. They were wearing the green headscarves frequently worn by members of Hamas. Both men were armed with rifles.

Cohen ran for cover. Soon dozens more militants had entered the kibbutz. Looking out of the window of his home, seventy-year-old Amit Solvy saw the Hamas fighters flood into the Be'eri streets. "I saw three or four white trucks pull up and Hamas people getting down from them," says Solvy. "They instructed people where to go. Together with Hamas, there were also a lot of young people with knives, machetes and bags to loot."[12] The militants fanned out throughout the kibbutz, breaking into homes and murdering occupants, then looting the homes of their possessions as well as vandalizing the properties. Cars were set on fire.

Kibbutzim in Israel typically have security teams—residents who are trained to repel terrorist attacks. Be'eri did have its own security team; soon after the attack began, the Be'eri security team members grabbed their weapons and ran into the streets to confront the attackers. But they were soon overwhelmed—about 150 Hamas fighters were believed to have entered the kibbutz that morning. One security team member, Yoel, was struck by a bullet fired by a Hamas militant. He crawled into an alleyway but then saw an object bounce nearby. "It was a hand grenade," he says. Yoel got to his feet and tried to run away but was hit with shrapnel from the explosion. He says, "While I was running it exploded and I was flying."[13] Miraculously, Yoel survived his wounds.

Friends and family are overcome by grief at a funeral for a couple who were killed by Hamas at Kibbutz Be'eri. Hamas killed about eighty residents of the kibbutz and abducted another thirty.

But many others in Be'eri did not. About eighty residents of the kibbutz—about 10 percent of the community's residents—were killed in the assault. Another thirty members of the kibbutz were captured and taken back to Gaza as hostages. Some forty homes in the kibbutz were destroyed by the Hamas militants.

Locked Away from Food and Water

Living near the kibbutz, Menachem Klemenson heard news reports of the attacks throughout Israel and suspected that Be'eri would be a target. Some of Klemenson's relatives were residents of the kibbutz. He called his brother, Elhanan, an officer in the IDF reserves—which is composed of former active-duty soldiers who can be recalled to service if they are needed. Menachem enlisted Elhanan to help save the residents of Be'eri. The two men donned bulletproof vests, armed themselves with firearms, and drove to Be'eri.

They found themselves wading into a chaotic scene. The Klemensons rushed to the aid of kibbutz residents, helping them find shelter in safe rooms. As night fell on the kibbutz, the Klemensons locked themselves into a safe room with many of the kibbutz residents. But even in the safe rooms, the kibbutz residents were in danger. Locked away without food, water, or ventilation, some died in their safe rooms while the carnage continued outside. "Some people were cooked alive inside their safe rooms because of the heat," says Menachem Klemenson. "We saw it."[14]

Some of the victims of the attack on Be'eri were children. Itzik Itah, commander of a volunteer civilian search and rescue unit, said his team arrived in Be'eri around midday on October 9 to help in the search for survivors. Entering the bedroom of one home, Itah said he found the bodies of two children whose skulls had been crushed. Each had knife wounds in their bodies. Their parents lay dead nearby, he said, each with similar wounds. "The dog was alive," Itah says. "It sat there on the bed next to the children and wouldn't move from the bed."[15]

In the days following the October 7 attack, Israeli military officials estimated that nearly three thousand Hamas terrorists had

Psytrance and the Attack on Supernova

During the early morning hours of October 7, 2023, Hamas targeted the Supernova music festival, raining bombs down on the event and sending armed militants onto the festival grounds to kill and kidnap attendees. Ironically, Supernova was a festival dedicated to a style of music known as psytrance, which features pulsing beats that listeners find calming. Psytrance fans are known to be peaceful and loving individuals.

Adam B. Coleman, a columnist for the *New York Post*, believes Hamas targeted the Supernova festival specifically because the militants believed the attendees would be easy targets. He says Hamas knew the psytrance fans would be unarmed and unable to defend themselves. He says, "The people who typically attend [psytrance] events are new-age hippie types, who appreciate humanity from all walks of life. They are among the most peaceful people you'd ever encounter—and that's partly why they were a perfect target for Hamas terrorists. I cannot help but see the symbolism attached to Hamas' attack on these unarmed, peaceful people."

Adam B. Coleman, "The Israeli Music Festival Hamas Slaughtered Had Its Roots in Peace and Love," *New York Post*, October 12, 2023. https://nypost.com.

crossed the border into Israel from Gaza, killing some twelve hundred people and taking more than two hundred hostages back to Gaza with them. The hostages ranged from elderly citizens to very young children. Moreover, following the attack many of the dead were identified as women who had been partially disrobed by their attackers—indicating that they had been raped by the militants before they were murdered. In March 2024 a UN investigation confirmed the charge that many victims of Hamas had been sexually assaulted before they were murdered.

Just the First Step Toward Israel's Destruction

In the aftermath of the October 7 attack, Ghazi Hamad—a Hamas senior leader—said the assault on Israel was just the first step in his organization's plan to destroy the Jewish state and replace it with a Palestinian state. In an interview with a Lebanese television station, later translated and published by the Middle East Media Research Institute, he said, "Israel is a country that has no place on our land. We must remove it because it constitutes a security, military and political catastrophe to the Arab and Islamic nations. We are not ashamed to

> "Israel is a country that has no place on our land."[16]
>
> —Ghazi Hamad, a leader of Hamas

Hamas senior leader Ghazi Hamad (pictured during a media interview in late October 2023), described his group's assault on Israel as just the first step in their plan to destroy the Jewish state and replace it with a Palestinian state.

say this. . . . We must teach Israel a lesson, and we will do it twice and three times."[16]

In that same interview, Hamad further acknowledged that Hamas fully expected a forceful response by Israel—a response that would likely have dire effects for Palestinians in Gaza. "Will we have to pay a price?" he asked. "Yes, and we are ready to pay it. We are called a nation of martyrs, and we are proud to sacrifice martyrs."[17]

The Iron Dome

As Hamad promised, during the ensuing months further attacks were launched by Hamas against Israel. In early 2024, IDF officials reported that since October 7 Hamas had launched some twelve thousand missiles toward Israel. Most of these missiles were destroyed before they reached their targets.

For years, Israel has maintained an elaborate antimissile system known as the Iron Dome. The nation's defense system is able to identify enemy missiles fired toward the nation, then respond by launching its own missiles toward the incoming rockets. The system enables the IDF to take out enemy missiles in the sky, destroying them before they hit their targets.

Still, despite the success of the Iron Dome, some of those Hamas missiles proved deadly. On October 7 the Iron Dome did not prevent all the Hamas missiles from hitting targets in Israel. And in the month following the initial October 7 attack, the IDF reported that the Hamas missile attacks had killed fifteen Israelis and injured about seven hundred others. The new attacks hardened the resolve of Israeli leaders to hit back hard against Hamas. Said Daniel Hagari, the Israeli military spokesperson, "If we don't diminish Hamas' rocket-firing capabilities, Hamas will continue firing rockets at Israelis."[18]

Because of the continued threat of attacks by Hamas, by the end of 2023 some two hundred thousand Israelis had been ordered to evacuate their homes. These were mostly people who lived within a few miles of Israel's borders with Gaza or with Lebanon to the north. Many of the displaced Israelis moved in with friends and family members living near the interior of the country. Others found refuge with friends and relatives in other countries. And many were provided with shelter by the Israeli government, typically in vacant hotel rooms throughout the country.

Never Again

A day after the October 7 attack, Israeli prime minister Benjamin Netanyahu addressed his nation. He declared a state of war against Hamas and said Israel would use its formidable military to attack Gaza and eliminate the militant group. "We will destroy them and we will forcefully avenge this dark day that they have forced on the State of Israel and its citizens," he said. "All of the places which Hamas is deployed, hiding and operating in . . . we will turn them into rubble."[19]

Israel is a nation founded in the aftermath of the Holocaust, in which 6 million Jews were murdered by the Nazis. During Israel's early years, the concept of "never again" was ingrained into the culture of Israelis—and Jews worldwide. It means that as long as Israel exists, never again would Jews be the targets of a campaign to rid them from the earth. Netanyahu's message to the people of Israel carried that message—that any attempt to eliminate the Jewish people would be met with a relentless and deadly response.

CHAPTER THREE

Israel Strikes Back

> "We are embarking on a long and difficult war. The war was forced upon us by a murderous attack by Hamas."
>
> —Benjamin Netanyahu, Israeli prime minister
>
> Quoted in Hadas Gold, "Israel Is 'Embarking on a Long and Difficult War,' Israeli Prime Minister Says," CNN, October 7, 2023. www.cnn.com.

Israel's response to the October 7 attack was swift and incendiary. In the first hours after Netanyahu declared war against Hamas, more than eight hundred targets in Gaza were hit by Israeli missiles. These strikes caused widespread destruction and killed hundreds of Gaza residents.

After the initial wave of missile launches, the IDF advised the more than 1 million citizens of Gaza City and nearby communities in the north to leave the region and head south. The Israeli military believed that large cells of Hamas militants were based in Gaza City. The IDF aimed to wipe out the Hamas cells with a fierce barrage of missiles as well as ground assaults. Shortly after the IDF began raining missiles down on Gaza City, Netanyahu made it clear what he intended to accomplish with the assault. He said:

> I've set three war goals. The first is to release the hostages. The second is to destroy Hamas. And the third is to ensure that Gaza does not pose a threat to Israel in the future. And obviously, the three are intertwined.... We can't leave Hamas in place.... Total victory is important to achieve the war goal of destroying Hamas, releasing the hostages, and ensuring that Gaza doesn't pose a threat.[20]

The missile attack was relentless. Within days entire neighborhoods of Gaza City as well as nearby communities were reduced to rubble. Mahmoud Jamal, a thirty-one-year-old taxi driver who lived in Beit Hanoun in the northern Gaza Strip, heeded Netanyahu's warning to head south. As he left his hometown, soon arriving in Gaza City, he passed through neighborhoods that had already been leveled by missile strikes. "When I left, I couldn't tell which street or intersection I was passing," says Jamal. In the neighborhoods he drove through, the taxi driver says he could not help but notice that towering apartment buildings in those areas of Gaza City were no longer standing. All that remained was rubble. Mkhaimer Abusada, a political science professor at Al-Azhar University in Gaza City who fled the region shortly after the missile attack commenced, noted, "The north of Gaza has been turned into one big ghost town. People have nothing to return to."[21]

> "Total victory is important to achieve the war goal of destroying Hamas, releasing the hostages, and ensuring that Gaza doesn't pose a threat."[20]
>
> —Benjamin Netanyahu, prime minister of Israel

Shortly after Israeli prime minister Benjamin Netanyahu declared war and vowed to destroy Hamas, Israeli missiles began striking Gaza. Netanyahu is pictured speaking at the United Nations a few weeks before the Hamas attack.

When pressed by the international media, IDF leaders insisted that the strikes on Gaza City residential neighborhoods were necessary because Israeli intelligence had detected activities by militants in those communities. Said an IDF spokesperson, "Hamas operates nearby, underneath, and within densely populated areas as a matter of routine operational practice. As part of the IDF's operations, it [has] been carrying out strikes on military targets, as well as locating and destroying infrastructure when imperatively required to achieve the goals of the war."[22]

Discovery of the Tunnels

To fulfill Netanyahu's vow to eliminate Hamas, the IDF knew it would take more than a barrage of missiles. On October 13—six days after the Hamas attack—Israeli soldiers crossed into Gaza prepared to engage the Hamas militants in street battles. Shortly after 6:00 p.m. that day, a vast invading force of tanks, armored vehicles, bulldozers, infantry soldiers, and other military personnel crossed into Gaza from several directions. Israeli forces encountered resistance from armed Hamas militants. Outnumbered and facing superior firepower, most of those militants were killed.

The mission of the IDF ground troops involved much more than just killing and capturing Hamas militants. As they made their way through Gaza City, the Israeli forces searched for the entranceways to a vast array of tunnels beneath the city streets.

For years the Mossad had been gathering intelligence on Hamas and had learned that the organization maintained its headquarters in tunnels beneath the streets of Gaza City and other nearby communities. As the war continued, IDF soldiers uncovered various entrances to the tunnels and concluded that there may have been as many as 400 miles (644 km) of tunnels snaking beneath communities in the Gaza Strip. According to Israeli military leaders, many of those tunnels had been dug under hospitals and schools in the belief that Israel would not launch missile strikes at facilities where ill and injured people were being treated or schoolchildren were taking classes.

Street Fighting

In its response to the October 7, 2023, attack by Hamas, the IDF rained missiles down on Gaza City and other communities in the Gaza Strip. But street battles between IDF soldiers and Hamas fighters were also significant in the conflict. By the end of 2023, it was clear the Israelis—armed with modern tanks and other armored vehicles—held the advantage in street warfare. At the time, the IDF reported a total of 127 casualties within its ranks. But the IDF also reported that it had killed some seven thousand Hamas militants in street combat.

In an interview with the news service Reuters, an anonymous Hamas leader insisted, though, that his organization would ordinarily expect to hold the advantage in street combat in Gaza City and other communities. The Hamas leader pointed out that its members are familiar with the streets and neighborhoods of Gaza communities, meaning they know of the most strategic locations to initiate surprise attacks. Still, the Hamas leader conceded, the militant group lacked the superior weapons of the IDF. Said the Hamas leader, "There is a huge discrepancy between our power and their power, we don't fool ourselves."

Quoted in Dan Williams et al., "Hamas Turns Gaza Streets into Deadly Maze for Israeli Troops," Reuters, December 17, 2023. www.reuters.com.

The IDF even discovered one tunnel snaking under a building that housed the United Nations Relief and Works Agency (UNRWA). The UNRWA oversees programs to provide food and other aid to impoverished people. (The UNRWA office had been established in Gaza—long regarded as an impoverished territory—well before the outbreak of the war.) An IDF spokesperson identified the tunnel as a power control station, directing electrical power to nearby tunnels in Gaza City. Leading a tour of the tunnel for journalists, an IDF colonel said, "Twenty meters above us is the UNRWA headquarters. This is the electricity room, you can see all around here. The batteries, the [electrical wiring] on walls, everything is conducted from here, all the energy for the tunnels which you walked through are powered from here."[23]

The IDF also suspected that some of the tunnels led outside of Gaza into Egypt, which enabled the militant group to secretly obtain weapons and supplies from sources outside the Gaza Strip. The government of Egypt does not recognize Hamas as the governing body of Gaza, nor does it supply Hamas with military or financial aid. Nevertheless, Hamas is known to have embedded agents in Egypt tasked with procuring arms and supplies and then secretly sending them through the tunnels into Gaza and the hands of Hamas militants. As long ago as 2009, the Washington Institute for Near East Policy, a Washington, DC–based group that studies international affairs, reported, "The arms travel overland to Egypt, through a variety of routes that cross Yemen, Eritrea, Ethiopia, and South Africa and eventually meet in Sudan, where they are moved to Egypt's Sinai desert. After the materiel enters the Sinai, it is transferred into Gaza via tunnels underneath . . . [the part of] the Gaza-Egypt border that runs through the city of Rafah."[24]

Soon after entering Gaza, the IDF soldiers found large caches of weapons stored in many tunnels. For example, in a network of tunnels beneath the central Gaza Strip town of Bureij, IDF soldiers found workshops dedicated to the construction of missiles. Within the workshops, the soldiers reported finding components of rockets, including long steel tubes as well as explosive shells intended to be attached to the tubes. Moreover,

In November 2023 Israeli soldiers scour Gaza for Hamas fighters. They were also searching for the entrances to a vast array of tunnels built by Hamas beneath the Palestinian territory.

A Tragic Error

In December 2023 Israeli forces mistakenly killed three hostages who had escaped captivity. Samer Al-Talalka, Alon Shamriz, and Yotam Haim, who were all in their twenties—had escaped captivity after a firefight between IDF soldiers and Hamas militants. After killing the Hamas fighters, the IDF soldiers moved on, not realizing Hamas had been holding three hostages nearby.

The three men had made their way out of the building where they had been held and for the next five days wandered through the streets of Gaza City, hoping to avoid recapture. Eventually, they encountered IDF soldiers. As they approached the Israeli military unit, the IDF soldiers mistook the former hostages for militants and opened fire—killing all three.

IDF colonel Jonathan Conricus said the soldiers who fired on Al-Talalka, Shamriz, and Haim were clearly on edge, believing militants could approach them at any time. "There is a direct link between the sad and very unfortunate mistake in killing those Israeli former hostages and the other ambush incidents," said Conricus. "It's super important to understand the psyche and the combat environment these soldiers are in."

Quoted in Anna Schecter, "How 3 Israeli Hostages Tried to Save Themselves, Only to Be Killed by Their Own Military," NBC News, December 22, 2023. www.nbcnews.com.

---

the IDF soldiers found vertical shafts within the network of tunnels that they suspected were used to launch the missiles toward Israel. Said Daniel Hagari, the IDF spokesperson, "In one place you make the rockets, another place you launch."[25] Also within the tunnels below Bureij, Hagari said, the IDF soldiers found stockpiles of mortar shells, which are small explosives that are launched from the ground, typically aimed at targets no more than five miles away.

The Israeli military claimed its tactics severely crippled Hamas. When IDF forces found arms and munitions stored inside the tunnels it meant those weapons were no longer at the disposal of the Hamas militants. A month after the first Israeli troops entered Gaza, the IDF announced its soldiers had seized nearly 1,500 hand grenades and similar explosives, 760 rocket-propelled grenades (small missiles fired by mobile rocket launchers), 427 explosive belts (typically used by suicide bombers), 375 rifles and handguns, and 106 rockets and missiles fired by stationary launch devices.

Searching for the Hostages

There was another reason for the IDF's focus on the tunnels: the IDF suspected that the hostages kidnapped on October 7 were being held prisoner in those tunnels. That suspicion was confirmed on January 21, 2024, when Israeli soldiers discovered a tunnel just over a half mile (1 km) in length beneath the city of Khan Younis. Inside were five narrow cells behind metal bars, complete with toilets, mattresses, and even drawings by a child hostage who had been held captive there. By this time the hostages had been moved elsewhere, but there were Hamas fighters in the tunnel. Said Hagari, "The soldiers entered the tunnel where they encountered terrorists, engaging in a battle that ended with the elimination of the terrorists."[26]

Meanwhile, on the streets above those tunnels, the combat was often fierce. By mid-January 2024, as the conflict passed the one-hundred-day mark, the IDF was routinely striking numerous communities in Gaza. The city of Khan Younis was hit particularly hard as missiles rained down on the community for several days, followed by an invasion by IDF ground troops.

At the time of the October 7 attack, the IDF estimated that Hamas fighters numbered thirty-five thousand to forty thousand. By February 2024 Israeli military leaders estimated that half of those fighters had been killed in missile attacks or street battles.

Supplies of Food and Fuel Cut Off

Israel employed more than missiles and ground troops in its efforts to cripple Hamas. Soon after the war commenced, Israel targeted power plants and fuel supplies. Shipments of food and medicine into Gaza were also cut off. To carry out the strategy, IDF soldiers manned posts at border crossings, stopping shipments of supplies from entering Gaza.

By limiting the supplies of food, medicine, gasoline, diesel fuel, and electricity into the Gaza Strip, Israel believed the Hamas militants would be further weakened, hampering their ability to wage combat. "No electricity, no food, no water, no fuel,"[27] declared Israeli defense minister Yoav Gallant just two days after the October 7 Hamas attack.

A single power plant located in the city of Deir al-Balah, along the coast of the Mediterranean Sea in central Gaza, supplies all of the Gaza Strip's electrical power. The diesel fuel that enables the plant to generate electricity is either trucked by land or shipped by sea. But the IDF blockade of the Gaza Strip halted deliveries both by land and sea.

On October 11—four days after the initial Hamas attack—the Deir al-Balah plant ran out of diesel fuel, forcing the plant to shut down. Virtually the entire Gaza Strip was now without power. Some homes and commercial properties were equipped with their own diesel-powered generators that produced electricity, but within days those generators ran out of fuel as well. Soon, neighborhoods that had remained standing amid the missile strikes were nevertheless in complete darkness at night.

> "No electricity, no food, no water, no fuel."[27]
>
> —Yoav Gallant, Israeli defense minister

Israeli airstrikes destroyed much of the Gaza Strip. The southern city of Khan Younis (pictured in April 2024) was hit particularly hard.

The IDF used the cover of darkness to launch numerous strikes at Hamas targets. "Nights here in Gaza are scary as hell," said twenty-six-year-old Gaza City resident Omar Alnajjar. "You are blinded. You don't see anything. Whenever you're going to bed or walking or sitting, there is always shaking. The building is shaking."[28]

> "Nights here in Gaza are scary as hell. You are blinded. You don't see anything."[28]
>
> —Omar Alnajjar, Gaza City resident

Within the first week of the war, some 250,000 Gaza residents were displaced by the fighting, with no homes to provide shelter, no electricity, and little food and water available to them. Soon, the number of Gaza civilians displaced by the war would grow to more than 1 million. Emboldened by the IDF's success against the Hamas militants, and despite the suffering of the Gaza civilians, Netanyahu vowed to continue the war until all Hamas militants had been eliminated. Addressing a meeting of his party's leaders, Netanyahu said, "Our goal is a complete victory over Hamas. . . . We must not end the war before then."[29]

CHAPTER FOUR

The Humanitarian Crisis

> "We are nine people in a tent of two meters by one meter. We have bought this camping tent ourselves; no-one helped us or provided it. Life is difficult and humiliating; the word humiliating is not even close to describing it."
>
> —Umm Omar, who fled with her family to Rafah from northern Gaza
>
> Quoted in Tim Lister and Kareem Khadder, "'What Kind of Life Is This?' Dire Conditions in Increasingly Cramped Southern Gaza," CNN, December 30, 2023. www.cnn.com.

Since the start of the war, Palestinian Americans Tariq Hamouda and his wife, Manal—residents of Maple Grove, Minnesota—had been in close contact with their many relatives living in Gaza. As the war raged on, they learned that their family members had taken shelter together in three neighboring homes owned by Manal's family in Gaza City.

Unlike many of the impoverished citizens of Gaza, members of Manal's family—her maiden name is Saqallah—were quite prosperous. Four of her brothers were physicians who operated one of Gaza City's busiest eye care practices. When the IDF missiles started raining down on Gaza City, the Saqallahs invited their relatives throughout the city to take shelter in the three neighboring homes they owned. But on October 19, 2023, IDF missiles hit the three homes. Forty-two members of the Saqallah family were killed in the blasts. The victims included all four of the physicians as well as a three-month-old baby and a seventy-seven-year-old grandparent. "Their kids, their grandkids were in [the same] building," says Tariq Hamouda. "They all got killed."[30]

Another family member, Manal's cousin Eyad Abu Shaban, resides in Boca Raton, Florida. Abu Shaban says he kept in close contact with his family members in Gaza and knows they had nothing to do with Hamas. "We have no Hamas members [in our family]," says Abu Shaban. "They're just ordinary people: doctors and grandmothers and grandfathers and uncles and aunts and children. . . . It's not one, two, three, or four—it is 42 members, it's really hard to cope with."[31]

As the war progressed, other families in Gaza suffered similar losses. In the early days of the war, as the missiles started falling on Gaza, many family members lost their homes. Surviving members of the same families came together to share homes because there were few places available to house the refugees. When the missile waves continued, it was not uncommon to see whole families virtually wiped out by the blasts.

On October 15, 2023—two days after Israeli forces crossed into Gaza—an apartment building where eighteen-year-old Dima al-Lamdani and members of her family were living was hit by a rocket. Seventeen members of al-Lamdani's family died in the blast. Al-Lamdani survived the blast—she was buried in the rubble but rescued by neighbors who rushed to aid the victims. Members of the al-Lamdani family lived in a northern Gaza community and, in the early days of the war, heeded the IDF warning to flee to southern Gaza. The al-Lamdani family believed they were safe in the southern Gaza home of a family friend. But then an IDF missile hit the apartment building where they believed they had found a safe shelter. Now al-Lamdani realizes she must live the remainder of her life without the cherished members of her family. "I am crumbled now. No dreams, no hopes, no plans. I can't imagine my life without my mother and sister and father," she said. "The Israeli forces betrayed us. There is no place that is safe."[32]

> "I am crumbled now. No dreams, no hopes, no plans. I can't imagine my life without my mother and sister and father."[32]
>
> —Dima al-Lamdani, who lost seventeen members of her family in an IDF attack

Overcome by grief, family and friends mourn the deaths of the Saqallah family. Forty-two members of the family who were sheltering together in three neighboring homes in Gaza City died in an Israeli airstrike.

Since the dawn of civilization, warfare has been a part of human culture, occurring on every populated continent on earth. But whether the wars have been waged in the Middle East in the twenty-first century or over past centuries in Europe, Asia, North America, or South America, there has always been one fact that connects the conflicts: civilians suffer the most. Says political scientist and author Marcus Schulzke, "If there is anything so fixed and unchanging that it can be regarded as inherent to war, then it is certainly that war causes immense human suffering. . . . [Civilians] suffer innumerable physical and psychological injuries. They are killed and incapacitated. They lose friends and family members. Their homes and workplaces are destroyed."[33]

Destruction Throughout Gaza

In 2023 and 2024 nowhere was that fact truer than in the Gaza Strip. Soon after the IDF started launching missiles into Gaza, news footage showed entire neighborhoods in Gaza City and

Why Did Egypt Refuse to Accept Refugees?

When Russia attacked Ukraine in February 2022, millions of Ukrainians fled to neighboring countries such as Poland, where they received help as refugees. After Israel responded to the Hamas attack on its people in October 2023, hundreds of thousands of Gaza residents were prevented from crossing into other countries such as Egypt, where they might find temporary refuge. Why were Palestinians from Gaza refused safe haven in Egypt, which shares a border with Gaza?

Egypt gave several reasons for this. One was fear that Israel would target their citizens if it suspected that Hamas fighters had crossed into Egypt along with civilians fleeing the violence. Another reason cited was concern that an influx of a million or more Palestinian refugees would overtax Egypt's ability to feed and house the refugees. Egypt also expressed concern that Israel would prevent Palestinian refugees from returning to Gaza once the war ended—something many Gaza residents also feared. Said Egyptian foreign minister Sameh Shoukry, "We are proud that we have always supported our brethren. But we hope that other countries will also bear the share of the burden, and provide for vulnerable communities the necessary support. I think those who have greater resources should probably bear greater responsibilities."

Quoted in Lee Ying Shan, "Egypt Does Not See Why Country Should 'Bear Solely' the Responsibility for Gaza's Refugee Influx," CNBC, October 18, 2023. www.cnbc.com.

---

other communities completely leveled by the blasts. And in the aftermath of each blast, bodies of civilians were found buried under the remnants of the buildings where the victims were caught by the missile strikes.

By early 2024 images obtained through satellites orbiting in space revealed that at least half the buildings in the Gaza Strip—homes, schools, workplaces, stores, and other structures—had been leveled by the Israeli missile strikes. Corey Scher, a graduate student at the City University of New York, helped analyze the satellite imagery. Scher says he has worked on similar projects—using satellite imagery to assess the destruction caused in Ukrainian cities due to Ukraine's war with Russia, as well as the damage in the Syrian city of Aleppo caused by civil war in that country from 2012 to 2016. Scher says the destruction in Gaza far exceeds the devastation suffered in Aleppo as well as the cities in Ukraine. He says, "We've done work over Ukraine, we've also looked at Aleppo and other cities, but the extent and the pace of damage [in Gaza] is remarkable. I've never seen this much damage appear so quickly."[34]

Fleeing Northern Gaza

Many civilians hoping to escape the missile strikes and street fighting heeded the IDF's warning to flee northern Gaza. Within weeks, the city of Rafah in southern Gaza was overflowing with refugees. Prior to the war the city's population was reported at about three hundred thousand residents. After the IDF commenced the attack on northern Gaza, the population of Rafah swelled to more than 1.5 million people.

Most of the refugees found no secure shelters awaiting them. Many lived in tent camps that were established throughout the city. Many refugees lived in their vehicles. Many lived on the streets. "We're exhausted. Seriously, we're exhausted," said Johan al-Hawajri, who fled to Rafah from his home in northern Gaza. "Israel can do whatever it wants. I'm sitting in my tent. I'll die in my tent."[35] Al-Hawajri shared his tent with thirty members of his family.

Facing Food Shortages

No matter where they went—whether they stayed in their houses or relocated to other parts of Gaza—residents faced dire living conditions. Even before the war, Gaza was regarded as an impoverished territory that relied heavily on international relief organizations to provide food, medical supplies, fuel, and other necessities. After the war started, these organizations rushed aid to Gaza but were stopped at the border crossings by the IDF. When Israel cut off these supplies, aid organizations and medical personnel warned of a growing threat of hunger, disease, and death among the civilian population. In December 2023 an international aid organization known as the Integrated Food Security Phase Classification released a report stating that 100 percent of the population of Gaza—some 2.2 million people—were suffering from malnutrition. Says Aaron Brent, head of a program sponsored by the international relief group CARE to deliver food to Gaza:

> Innocent families caught up in the fighting will face greater risks of being killed as hunger forces them to . . . wait in

long lines outside bakeries, further exposing them to the fighting. . . . We know from our experience that women and girls usually eat last and least. Severe hunger will have even greater impacts as it negatively affects immune health and exposes them to nutrition-related illnesses, while infectious diseases are spreading rampantly.[36]

Soon after the war erupted, the home of Yousef Hammash and his family in northern Gaza was destroyed in an IDF bombardment. Hammash and his family fled to Khan Younis, where they found shelter in the home of a relative. After arriving in Khan Younis, Hammash woke at 4:00 a.m. each day to stand in a line at a nearby bakery. After waiting in line for two hours, Hammash says, he was given two small pieces of bread to take home and share with his family—including his wife, two children, mother, three sisters, and two nephews. Says Hammash, "Everyone is traumatized, especially the children."[37]

> "Everyone is traumatized, especially the children."[37]
>
> —Yousef Hammash, Palestinian refugee

Lack of drinkable water has also become a huge problem. Prior to the war, Gaza relied on several desalination plants to provide drinkable water. Located along Gaza's Mediterranean Sea coastline, the plants remove the salt from seawater, making the water drinkable. The water is then fed into pipelines that supply Gaza communities. But soon after the war started, most of the plants had to shut down because they were out of fuel needed to run the machinery in the plants. This meant that drinkable water was soon in short supply throughout the Gaza Strip. In late December 2023, one of the few desalination plants still operating in Gaza was located in Rafah. When refugees arrived in the city, the Rafah plant was soon overwhelmed and unable to meet the demand. Yousef Abdul Salam Yaseen, the manager of the Rafah desalination plant, says the facility was not designed to provide water to so many consumers. "We can't produce enough water for them," he says. "But we are doing everything we can."[38]

In its war against Hamas, Israel cut off food, water, and electricity in the Gaza Strip. Desperate for food, in March 2024, children in Rafah in southern Gaza hold up empty bowls as they wait to receive food.

Hospitals Shut Down

In addition to the scarcity of food and water, the conflict led to little medical care being available to the citizens of the Gaza Strip. By early 2024, with some seventy thousand Gaza citizens sustaining injuries due to the conflict, the hospitals in the Gaza Strip soon became overwhelmed. Staffing became an immediate issue: in some cases doctors, nurses, and other staff members fled from communities that were under assault, leaving hospitals understaffed. And in some cases doctors, nurses, and other hospital workers lost their lives in IDF assaults.

With electrical power cut off to Gaza, hospitals were unable to operate the numerous devices needed to provide lifesaving care to injured people. Ventilators and respirators that provide oxygen to people who suffer injuries to their lungs were now unavailable to the victims. X-ray devices and magnetic resonance imaging machines that assist doctors in identifying internal injuries could not

Hamas Hid Food in the Tunnels

The Israeli attack on Gaza left thousands of people homeless and near starvation, but soon after IDF soldiers entered the Gaza Strip, they found evidence that the Hamas militants were enjoying regular meals. After entering the Hamas tunnels, IDF soldiers found ample supplies of food, water, and fuel.

Intelligence experts concluded that Hamas had been planning the October 7 attack for years and in doing so anticipated the need for food, water, and fuel to maintain its combatants. And so Hamas stockpiled those supplies in anticipation of the fierce response by the Israelis to the October 7 attack—which included cutting off food, water, and fuel shipments into the Gaza Strip. Reported the *New York Times*, "Hamas has hundreds of thousands of gallons of fuel for vehicles and rockets; caches of ammunition, explosives and materials to make more; and stockpiles of food, water and medicine. . . . Hamas, which is estimated to number between 35,000 and 40,000, had enough stocked away to keep fighting for three to four months without resupply."

Matthew Rosenberg and Maria Abi-Habib, "As Gazans Scrounge for Food and Water, Hamas Sits on a Rich Trove of Supplies," *New York Times*, October 27, 2023. www.nytimes.com.

---

be employed because they require electricity to operate. Defibrillators, which are employed to restart hearts that have stopped beating, had to be shut down. Numerous other lifesaving devices were no longer available to the victims of the IDF attacks.

Other challenges soon became evident. With no gasoline available in Gaza, ambulances had no fuel to reach injured people. Medications, bandages, and blood from donors fell into short supply as well. Humanitarian groups attempted to provide assistance to the hospitals, but their efforts fell well short of providing the aid that was needed. In January 2024, Irfan Galaria, a Virginia-based surgeon, joined a humanitarian mission sponsored by MedGlobal, an Illinois-based group that responds to international medical crises. Galaria and other American physicians traveled to Gaza. Galaria, who spent ten days at a hospital in Khan Younis, described his experience:

> I began work immediately, performing 10 to 12 surgeries a day, working 14 to 16 hours at a time. The operating room would often shake from the incessant bombings, some-

times as frequent as every 30 seconds. We operated in unsterile settings that would've been unthinkable in the United States. We had limited access to critical medical equipment: We performed amputations of arms and legs daily, using a Gigli saw, a Civil War–era tool, essentially a segment of barbed wire. Many amputations could've been avoided if we'd had access to standard medical equipment. It was a struggle trying to care for all the injured within the constructs of a healthcare system that has utterly collapsed.[39]

Prior to the war there were thirty-six hospitals in operation in Gaza. But as the IDF ramped up the bombardment, many of those facilities were either damaged by the attacks or simply closed because they lacked the staff members and supplies to treat patients. On February 29, 2024, the Al-Awda Hospital in

With electricity cut off and repeated missile strikes, Gaza hospitals and medical workers have struggled to provide treatment for ill and injured residents. In March 2024 doctors and nurses had little room to work in this hospital in southern Gaza.

the city of Jabalia was forced to shut down. It was the last functioning hospital that was still in operation in northern Gaza. Said Muhammad Salha, a physician at Al-Awda, "[The shutdown] will lead to a complete deprivation of basic health services for citizens, especially in light of the cessation of service by all hospitals in the north."[40]

As the war wore on, it became increasingly clear that innocent citizens of Gaza—and not the Hamas militants—were bearing the brunt of the pain, anguish, and loss that accompanied the IDF assault. Whole families had been wiped out in missile attacks. Refugees were forced to live in tents or on the streets. Vast portions of cities in Gaza had been reduced to rubble. Food, water, fuel, and medicine were scarce. By the spring of 2024, the only certainty for Gaza residents was continued suffering.

CHAPTER FIVE

The World Responds

> "There is no doubt that Israel had right on its side, in war terms, to decide to go on the offensive against Hamas. . . . What is not reasonable is the way they have conducted themselves, they have killed far too many people, and far too many people who are innocent Gazan citizens wrapped up in their attempts to kill Hamas terrorists."
>
> —Richard Dannatt, a member of Parliament and former head of the British army
>
> Quoted in Archie Mitchell and Bel Trew, "Calls Grow for Rishi Sunak to Stop UK Arms Trade to Israel Now," *The Independent*, April 5, 2024. www.independent.co.uk.

As Israeli missiles fell on the Gaza Strip, as Israeli soldiers and Hamas fighters engaged in street combat, as more than 1 million Gaza civilians were forced to flee their homes and hunger and disease, and as dozens of Israeli hostages were still being held, diplomats from several nations worked behind the scenes with the goal of achieving a ceasefire. Among the diplomats taking lead roles in the talks were officials from the United States, Egypt, and Qatar, who met with leaders from Israel and Hamas in an effort to end the fighting, free the hostages, and bring humanitarian aid to the civilians uprooted by the war.

But by the spring of 2024, after nearly six months of warfare, the diplomats had made little progress. Throughout the conflict, Netanyahu and other Israeli leaders remained firm in their resolve to eliminate Hamas, while leaders of the militant group insisted they would continue their efforts to wipe Israel off the map.

International diplomats could point to only one short-lived success: a brief ceasefire that commenced on November 24, 2023. Under the terms of this ceasefire, Hamas released 105 hostages—mostly women and children. In return, Israel agreed to release 180 Palestinians who had been held in Israeli prisons, charged with militant activities in Israel.

Among the Israeli hostages released in the prisoner exchange was Mia Schem, age twenty-one. Schem had been captured by Hamas at the Supernova music festival, where she sustained a gunshot wound to her arm. Schem confirmed that she had been held in a tunnel by Hamas, usually fed no more than a piece of bread a day during her captivity. She hardly slept during the six weeks of her captivity. "It's important to me to reveal the real situation about the people who live in Gaza, who they really are, and what I went through there," she said after her release. "I experienced hell. Everyone there are terrorists . . . there are no innocent civilians, not one."[41] Following the prisoner exchange, it was believed more than one hundred Israeli hostages remained in Hamas captivity.

> "Everyone there are terrorists . . . there are no innocent civilians, not one."[41]
>
> —Mia Schem, freed Israeli hostage

After the weeklong pause in fighting, the warfare recommenced on December 1. Israeli fighter jets were dispatched that day, firing missiles toward suspected Hamas enclaves throughout Gaza. Some of those missiles hit a refugee camp near the central Gaza city of Maghazi. "There was no warning at 7:00 a.m. It happened right after the so-called truce ended," says Abu Ziyad, a refugee at the camp. "It was full of innocent children and normal civilians."[42] Hamas responded by firing rockets into Israel. Witnesses in Israeli communities along the Gaza border reported seeing scores of bursts in the sky above—evidence that Israel's Iron Dome had intercepted the Hamas rockets.

Foreign Aid to Israel

Immediately after the Hamas attack, leaders of several nations expressed strong support for Israel. This included the United

US Secretary of State Antony Blinken (third from left) meets with Qatar's emir and prime minister in January 2024 to discuss ways to get aid to Gaza civilians, free Israeli hostages, and end the fighting. High-level talks have also taken place in other countries.

States. On October 10 President Joe Biden stated, "You know, there are moments in this life—and I mean this literally—when the pure, unadulterated evil is unleashed on this world. The people of Israel lived through one such moment this weekend. The bloody hands of the terrorist organization Hamas—a group whose stated purpose for being is to kill Jews. This was an act of sheer evil."[43]

Moreover, on October 18, 2023, Biden flew to Israel and met with Benjamin Netanyahu, pledging US support for the IDF assault on Hamas. In the eight decades since the founding of Israel, the United States has been regarded as the Middle Eastern nation's closest ally. And in no place has evidence of that alliance been greater than in the willingness of US officials to provide Israel with arms and other military aid. According to the Council on Foreign Relations—a New York City–based organization that studies international affairs—since the founding of Israel in 1948, the United States has provided the country

> "There are moments in this life—and I mean this literally—when the pure, unadulterated evil is unleashed on this world."[43]
>
> —Joe Biden, US president

Hate Spills Over

Hate speech and violence have spilled over onto American college campuses and city streets in connection with events taking place in the Middle East. Although many protests have been peaceful, some have devolved into hate speech. On the campuses of many American universities, Jewish students say they have been harassed because of their faith. Joe Gindi, a student at Rutgers University in New Jersey, reported that protesters screamed at him, "We don't want Zionists here!" This is a reference to the movement for statehood for the Jewish people in Israel, their ancestral homeland.

Hate-filled violence has also taken place. In November 2023 three young Palestinian men, all college students, were shot while walking on a street in Burlington, Vermont. The students were speaking Arabic, and two of them were wearing kaffiyehs—the traditional black and white scarves worn by men in parts of the Arab world. Two of the victims were expected to make full recoveries from their wounds, but one victim will never walk again. The alleged attacker, forty-eight-year-old Jason Eaton of Burlington, was charged with hate crimes in the shooting of the three men. Eaton pleaded not guilty. By the spring of 2024, he had yet to face trial.

Quoted in Anemona Hartocollis, "Jewish Students Describe Facing Antisemitism on Campus to Members of Congress," *New York Times*, March 1, 2024. www.nytimes.com.

---

with some $300 billion in aid. And most of that aid has gone toward beefing up Israel's military. Said a January 2024 report by the Council on Foreign Relations, "Nearly all US aid today goes to support Israel's military, the most advanced in the region."[44]

Other nations have also provided military assistance to Israel, among them Germany, Great Britain, France, and Australia. Following the October 7 attack by Hamas, German chancellor Olaf Scholz pledged his nation's support for Israel. Because of Germany's responsibility for the murders of Jews during the Holocaust, Scholz said, his country bears the perpetual obligation to support the Jewish people against their enemies. Said Scholz, "On the morning of 7 October, Israel woke up to a nightmare. . . . At this moment, there is only one place for Germany: alongside Israel."[45]

Support for Hamas

Over the years Hamas has also relied on aid from other governments. In Qatar, leaders of the oil-rich Arab nation have long expressed their sympathy for the plight of the Palestinian people and—despite Hamas's reputation as a militant organization—provided financial support for the group. According to Amos Gilad, a former official in the Israeli Ministry of Defense, since 2018 Qatar has provided Hamas with some $360 million per year in aid.

Hamas has also relied on Iran, another Middle Eastern nation, for significant assistance in aid. Iran—led by a fundamentalist Islamic regime—has maintained icy relations with Israel as well as the United States and other Western democracies for decades. According to US intelligence officials, Iran provides weapons to the Hamas militants as well as training in how to use the weapons. Shortly after the October 7 attack, Jonathan Finer, deputy national security adviser in the Biden administration, said, "What I can say without a doubt is that Iran is broadly complicit in these attacks. Iran has been Hamas's primary backer for decades. They have provided them weapons. They have provided them training. They have provided them financial support. And so, in terms of broad complicity, we are very clear about a role for Iran."[46]

Protests Erupt Around the World

By the time the war entered the spring of 2024, images of the humanitarian crisis in Gaza could not have been more vivid. Each day, news broadcasts of the devastation filled the airwaves in the United States and around the world. Diplomats grew more and more frustrated by the refusal of Netanyahu to negotiate with Hamas. In Washington, DC, reports surfaced indicating that Biden had grown frustrated with the Israeli prime minister. In an interview aired on the MSNBC network, Biden said, "[Netanyahu] must pay more attention to the innocent lives being lost as a consequence of the actions taken [in Gaza.] He's hurting Israel more than helping Israel. . . . It's contrary to what Israel stands for. And I think it's a big mistake."[47]

A significant swing in the US government's position toward Israel occurred on March 14, 2024, when Senator Chuck Schumer stood at the podium on the Senate floor and called for new elections to be staged in Israel with the goal of replacing Netanyahu as prime minister. A Democrat representing New York State, at the time Schumer was the majority leader in the Senate and therefore the most powerful senator in Congress. He also held the highest elective post in the US government ever achieved by a member of the Jewish faith. Schumer opened his remarks by recounting his long support for Israel but declared that no resolution to the conflict can be achieved until Netanyahu is replaced by an Israeli leader more willing to accept a two-state solution. Said Schumer, "At this critical juncture, I believe a new election is the only way to allow for a healthy and open decision-making process about the future of Israel."[48]

Moreover, soon after the IDF started its bombardment of Gaza, protests erupted around the world. These protests took place across the United States and in many European cities. Most protesters were demanding a ceasefire to protect civilians in Gaza. As the bombardment continued, the protests continued as well.

In New York City thousands of protesters gathered in the city's Washington Square Park to demand a ceasefire. Among the pro-

Thousands of protesters gather in Washington Square Park in New York City in March 2024. They demanded an immediate ceasefire by Israel.

testers was film star Susan Sarandon, who spoke during the March 2, 2024, rally. "There are hundreds more across Manhattan, hundreds of thousands across the US, millions globally who are standing for Palestine for justice, for a ceasefire,"[49] Sarandon said during the rally.

> "There are hundreds more across Manhattan, hundreds of thousands across the US, millions globally who are standing for Palestine for justice, for a ceasefire."[49]
>
> —Susan Sarandon, American film star

Supplies Trickle into Gaza

While diplomats from the United States, Egypt, and Qatar were unable to negotiate a long-term ceasefire, they eventually convinced Israel to permit humanitarian aid to enter Gaza. Initially, groups such as CARE attempted to respond quickly to the crisis in Gaza, but they soon found that their plans to truck food, water, medicine, and other supplies into the Gaza Strip had been halted by the IDF. Israeli officials said they were concerned that Hamas supporters outside the Gaza Strip would find ways to smuggle weapons into Gaza, hidden within the shipments of food. But critics countered that Israel was using starvation as a weapon—meaning that by denying food to Gaza civilians, the IDF was intentionally creating a hunger crisis to pressure Hamas to surrender. Charged the international aid group Human Rights Watch, "The Israeli government is using starvation of civilians as a method of warfare in the occupied Gaza Strip, which is a war crime. . . . Israeli forces are deliberately blocking the delivery of water, food, and fuel, while willfully impeding humanitarian assistance, apparently razing agricultural areas, and depriving the civilian population of objects indispensable to their survival."[50]

Diplomats from the United States and other nations pressured Israeli leaders to permit food, water, and medical supplies to enter Gaza. Finally, on October 21—just two weeks after the initial attack—Israel permitted the first aid trucks to enter Gaza through a crossing on the Egyptian border. Trucks had been parked at the border crossing for several days—officials estimated they were loaded with some 3,000 tons (2,722 metric tons) of food, water, and medicine. But on that initial day, the IDF permitted just twenty trucks to cross over into Gaza. Said the World Health Organization, an agency of the UN, "The supplies currently heading into Gaza will barely begin to address the escalating health needs as hostilities continue to grow. Much more is needed."[51]

Diplomats negotiating with Israel kept up the pressure, and finally, in March 2024, those efforts resulted in a US-backed plan to fly military cargo planes over the Gaza Strip and drop tons of food and other supplies by parachute into the territory. On March 2, 2024—the first day of the airdrop—US Air Force cargo planes dropped hundreds of bundles containing some forty thousand meals into the Gaza Strip. Video recorded by the crews aboard the cargo planes showed images of hundreds of civilians swarming around the packages as they floated to the ground. Soon after the airdrops commenced, the US military led a project to establish a temporary pier on Gaza's Mediterranean coast to enable supply ships to unload food, water, medical supplies, and other necessities for the Palestinian civilians suffering through the IDF assaults.

Humanitarian supplies are loaded onto a US Air Force aircraft in March 2024. The supplies were to be airdropped over Gaza. This was just one of several airdrops aimed at getting much needed help to the people of Gaza.

The War Widens Beyond Gaza

Throughout the Israel-Hamas War, violence was not confined to Gaza. In February 2024 an Israeli drone was dispatched to the neighboring country of Lebanon, where it fired on a vehicle traveling near the city of Jadra, about 37 miles (60 km) from the Israeli border. The IDF said the target of the strike was a Hamas leader, Basel Saleh, a passenger in the car. Saleh was reported to have only been injured in the strike.

Meanwhile, the conflict sparked attacks on commercial shipping in the nearby Red Sea by a militant group known as the Houthis, which is based in the Middle Eastern nation of Yemen. With missiles and drones believed to have been supplied by Iran, the Houthis launched several attacks on cargo ships crossing the Red Sea. By the spring of 2024 nearly thirty such attacks had been staged. Militaries from Israel, the United States, and other nations struck back at Houthi bases in Yemen, but sporadic attacks continued for several months. Said Eleonora Ardemagni, an analyst at the Milan, Italy–based Institute for International Political Studies, "Without a cease-fire in Gaza, the Houthis could be tempted to further escalate against US interests in the Red Sea and in the region."

Quoted in Jon Gambrell, "Attacks on Ships and US Drones Show Yemen's Houthis Can Still Fight Despite US-Led Airstrikes," Associated Press, February 20, 2024. https://apnews.com.

Deepening Hatred on All Sides

Despite diplomatic efforts, the war continued as Israel ramped up its attacks on Gaza. In March the IDF turned its attention to Rafah and other communities in southern Gaza that Israel believed were now harboring cells of Hamas militants. For months, the IDF had been advising citizens of northern Gaza to flee the region and head to southern Gaza. Now, with more than 1 million Palestinians crammed into existing homes and apartments or refugee camps in southern Gaza, Netanyahu was reported to be mulling over a full-scale barrage on Rafah. In the meantime, the IDF fired some missiles at targets in Rafah and nearby southern Gaza communities.

On March 2, 2024, a missile hit the home in Rafah where the family of Rania Abu Anza had been sheltering since the start of the war. The Palestinian woman lost fourteen relatives in the blast, including her husband, son, and daughter. "I screamed for my children and my husband," she says. "They were all dead. Their father took them and left me behind."[52]

By the spring of 2024, incidents such as the missile strike that robbed Abu Anza of her family had become all too common in the Israel-Hamas War. And even if diplomatic efforts to achieve a lasting ceasefire would ultimately prove successful, it was clear the deadly conflict sparked by the October 7 Hamas attack served only to deepen the hatred and mistrust harbored between the Israelis and Palestinians. Acts of terrorism and warfare will likely cast a long shadow over the region for years to come.

SOURCE NOTES

Introduction: A Long and Simmering Feud Turns Lethal

1. Quoted in Lori Hinnant and Sam McNeil, "'We Are Officially Hostages.' How the Israeli Kibbutz of Nir Oz Embodied Hamas' Hostage Strategy," Associated Press, December 5, 2023. https://apnews.com.
2. Quoted in Aya Batrawy, "A Gaza Woman Describes Trying to Keep Her Family Safe—and Alive," National Public Radio, November 29, 2023. www.npr.org.
3. Quoted in Times of Israel, "Taken Captive: Sagui Dekel-Chen Spotted First Incoming Terrorists," October 19, 2023. www.timesofisrael.com.

Chapter One: Seeds of the Conflict

4. Quoted in Ilan Ben Zion, "Netanyahu's Government Vows to Expand West Bank Settlements, Annex Occupied Territory," *PBS NewsHour*, December 28, 2022. www.pbs.org.
5. Quoted in Maayan Lubell, "Netanyahu Says No Palestinian State as Long as He's Prime Minister," Reuters, March 16, 2015. www.reuters.com.
6. Thomas L. Friedman, "What Is Happening to Our World?," *New York Times*, December 29, 2023. www.nytimes.com.

Chapter Two: Hamas Attacks

7. Quoted in David Browne et al., "They Wanted to Dance in Peace. And They Got Slaughtered," *Rolling Stone*, October 15, 2023. www.rollingstone.com.
8. Quoted in Browne et al., "They Wanted to Dance in Peace."
9. Quoted in Roger Cohen, "Slaughter at a Festival of Peace and Love Leaves Israel Transformed," *New York Times*, October 15, 2023. www.nytimes.com.
10. Quoted in Thomas Helm et al., "Hamas Launches Biggest Attack on Israel in Years," *The National*, October 7, 2023. www.thenationalnews.com.
11. Quoted in Beth Reece, "Trapped: Navy Reservist Escapes Israel After Hamas Attack," US Defense Logistics Agency, November 5, 2023. www.dla.mil.

12. Quoted in Stephen Grey et al., "Hunted by Hamas: 27 Hours of Slaughter and Survival Inside Israel's Kibbutz Be'eri," Reuters, November 3, 2023. www.reuters.com.
13. Quoted in Grey et al., "Hunted by Hamas."
14. Quoted in Grey et al., "Hunted by Hamas."
15. Quoted in Grey et al., "Hunted by Hamas."
16. Quoted in *Economic Times* (Mumbai, India), "Hamas Official Vows to 'Repeat' Oct. 7 Attack Repeatedly to Teach Israel a Lesson," November 2, 2023. https://economictimes.indiatimes.com.
17. Quoted in *Economic Times* (Mumbai, India), "Hamas Official Vows to 'Repeat' Oct. 7 Attack Repeatedly to Teach Israel a Lesson."
18. Quoted in Nadav Gavrielov, "Hamas and Other Militant Groups Are Firing Rockets into Israel Every Day," *New York Times*, January 2, 2024. www.nytimes.com.
19. Quoted in New Arab, "Israel's Netanyahu Vows to Make 'Rubble' of Hamas Hiding Places After Attack," October 8, 2023. www.newarab.com.

Chapter Three: Israel Strikes Back

20. Quoted in CBS News, "Transcript: Israeli Prime Minister Benjamin Netanyahu on 'Face the Nation,' February 25, 2024," February 25, 2024. www.cbsnews.com.
21. Quoted in Isabel Debre, "Gaza Has Become a Moonscape in War. When the Battles Stop, Many Fear It Will Remain Uninhabitable," Associated Press, November 23, 2023. https://apnews.com.
22. Quoted in Niels de Hoog et al., "How War Destroyed Gaza's Neighbourhoods—Visual Investigation," *The Guardian* (Manchester, UK), January 30, 2024. www.theguardian.com.
23. Quoted in Associated Press, "Israeli Military Alleges Hamas Made Use of Tunnels Under UN Agency's Main Office in Gaza City," CBC, February 10, 2024. www.cbc.ca.
24. Yoram Cohen and Matthew Levitt, "Hamas Arms Smuggling: Egypt's Challenge," Washington Institute for Near East Policy, March 2, 2009. www.washingtoninstitute.org.
25. Quoted in Ronen Zvulun, "Israeli Forces Say They Locate Large Underground Weapons Factory in Gaza," Reuters, January 8, 2024. www.reuters.com.
26. Quoted in Reuters, "Israeli Soldiers Uncover Gaza Tunnel That Once Held Hostages: Army," January 21, 2024. www.reuters.com.
27. Quoted in Isabel Kershner et al., "Israel Orders 'Siege' of Gaza; Hamas Threatens to Kill Hostages," *New York Times*, October 9, 2023. www.nytimes.com.

28. Quoted in Kiara Alfonseca and Somayeh Malekian, "'Scary as Hell': Gazan Describes Fearful Nights amid Israeli Airstrikes," ABC News, October 14, 2023. https://abcnews.go.com.
29. Quoted in Emanuel Fabian et al., "Israel Says Half Hamas Fighters Taken Out, Sinwar on Run, as PM Vows Victory in Months," Times of Israel, February 5, 2024. www.timesofisrael.com.

Chapter Four: The Humanitarian Crisis

30. Quoted in Ubah Ali and Davey Johnson, "Maple Grove Family Says 30 Members Killed in Gaza Strip," CBS News, October 20, 2023. www.cbsnews.com.
31. Quoted in Isabel Rosales et al., "Palestinian American Family Mourns 42 Relatives Killed in a Single Day in Gaza," CNN, November 4, 2023. www.cnn.com.
32. Quoted in Wafa Aludaini, "'Why Didn't We Die Together?': The Last Survivors of Three Gaza Families Speak," *The Guardian* (Manchester, UK), November 8, 2023. www.theguardian.com.
33. Marcus Schulzke, *Just War Theories and Civilian Casualties: Protecting the Victims of War*. Cambridge, UK: Cambridge University Press, 2017, p. 1.
34. Quoted in Daniele Palumbo et al., "At Least Half of Gaza's Buildings Damaged or Destroyed, New Analysis Shows," BBC, January 20, 2024. www.bbc.com.
35. Quoted in Najib Jobain and Lee Keath, "'I'll Die in My Tent:' Israel's Next Target in Gaza War Is Likely Rafah as Despair Spreads Through Population," *PBS NewsHour*, February 9, 2024. www.pbs.org.
36. Quoted in ReliefWeb, "Gaza: With 100 Percent of the Population Facing Hunger Crisis, Only a Ceasefire Can Prevent a Full Famine," December 21, 2023. https://reliefweb.int.
37. Quoted in Thomas Fuller and Vivian Yee, "First Humanitarian Aid Reaches a Hard-Pressed Gaza," *New York Times*, October 21, 2023. www.nytimes.com.
38. Quoted in Anas Baba and Scott Neuman. "There's a Water Crisis in Gaza That the End of Fighting Might Not Solve," National Public Radio, December 29, 2023. www.npr.org.
39. Irfan Galaria, "Opinion: I'm an American Doctor Who Went to Gaza. What I Saw Wasn't War—It Was Annihilation," *Los Angeles Times*, February 16, 2024. www.latimes.com.
40. Quoted in John Bacon and Jorge L. Ortiz, "Hospital Shut Down in Northern Gaza, Where Food Trucks Finally Arrive," *USA Today*, February 29, 2024. www.usatoday.com.

Chapter Five: The World Responds

41. Quoted in Amy Spiro and Michael Horovitz, "Freed Hostage Mia Schem: 'I Experienced Hell. There Are No Innocent Civilians in Gaza,'" Times of Israel, December 29, 2023. www.timesofisrael.com.
42. Quoted in Nick Schifrin et al., "War Returns to Gaza After Cease-Fire Between Israel and Hamas Ends," *PBS NewsHour*, December 1, 2023. www.pbs.org.
43. White House, "Remarks by President Biden on the Terrorist Attacks in Israel," October 10, 2023. www.whitehouse.gov.
44. Jonathan Masters and Will Merrow, "US Aid to Israel in Four Charts," Council on Foreign Relations, January 23, 2024. www.cfr.org.
45. Quoted in Andrew Tillett, "Albanese Slams Protest Targeting Israeli Hostages' Families," *Australian Financial Review* (Sydney, Australia), November 30, 2023. www.afr.com.
46. Quoted in Federal Government of Germany, "Germany Stands by Israel—and Is Seeking to Bring About a De-Escalation," December 22, 2023. www.bundesregierung.de.
47. Quoted in Barak Ravid, "Biden Breaks with Netanyahu but Sticks with Israel," Axios, March 10, 2024. www.axios.com.
48. Quoted in Times of Israel, "Full Text of Senator Chuck Schumer's Speech: 'Israeli Elections Are the Only Way,'" March 15, 2024. www.timesofisrael.com.
49. Quoted in NBC New York, "Police Arrest 11 Demonstrators at NYC Pro-Palestinian March After Chaotic Clash," March 3, 2024. www.nbcnewyork.com.
50. Quoted in ReliefWeb, "Israel: Starvation Used as Weapon of War in Gaza," December 18, 2023. https://reliefweb.int.
51. Quoted in Thomas Fuller and Vivian Yee, "First Humanitarian Aid Reaches a Hard-Pressed Gaza," *New York Times*, October 21, 2023. www.nytimes.com.
52. Quoted in Wafaa Shurafa and Samy Magdy, "Gaza Woman Mourns Deaths of Twin Babies, Husband in Bombing," *Philadelphia Inquirer*, March 4, 2024, p. A1.

FOR FURTHER RESEARCH

Books

Paola Caridi, *Hamas: From Resistance to Regime*. New York: Seven Stories, 2023.

Alan Dershowitz, *War Against the Jews: How to End Hamas Barbarism*. New York: Skyhorse, 2023.

Rashid Khalidi, *Hundred Years' War on Palestine: A History of Settler Colonialism and Resistance, 1917–2017*. New York: Picador, 2021.

Benjamin Netanyahu, *Bibi: My Story*. New York: Threshold Editions, 2022.

Amir Tibon, *The Gates of Gaza: A Story of Betrayal, Survival, and Hope in Israel's Borderlands*. Boston: Little, Brown, 2024.

Internet Sources

Wafa Aludaini, "'Why Didn't We Die Together?' The Last Survivors of Three Gaza Families Speak," *The Guardian* (Manchester, UK), November 8, 2023. www.theguardian.com.

David Browne et al., "They Wanted to Dance in Peace. And They Got Slaughtered," *Rolling Stone*, October 15, 2023. www.rollingstone.com.

Niels de Hoog et al., "How War Destroyed Gaza's Neighbourhoods—Visual Investigation," *The Guardian* (Manchester, UK), January 30, 2024. www.theguardian.com.

Stephen Grey et al., "Hunted by Hamas: 27 Hours of Slaughter and Survival Inside Israel's Kibbutz Be'eri," Reuters, November 3, 2023. www.reuters.com.

Patrick Kingsley and Ronen Bergman, "Under Shroud of Secrecy, Israel Invasion of Gaza Has Begun," *New York Times*, October 30, 2023. www.nytimes.com.

Organizations and Websites

American-Israeli Cooperative Enterprise (AICE)
Jewish Virtual Library
www.jewishvirtuallibrary.org
Established by the Chevy Chase, Maryland–based AICE, the website for the Jewish Virtual Library includes resources on Israel's history,

including an overview of internal politics in the Middle Eastern nation. By accessing the link for US & Israel, visitors can find articles illustrating the support provided by the United States for Israel since the nation's founding in 1948.

Arab America Institute: Palestine
www.aaiusa.org/palestine
Established by the Washington, DC–based organization that advocates for civil rights for Arab Americans, the website includes analyses of the negotiations to end the Israel-Hamas War. Among the articles available on the site is an analysis in the rise of hate crimes against Arab Americans since the start of the war.

European Council on Foreign Relations: Mapping Palestinian Politics
https://ecfr.eu/special/mapping_palestinian_politics/palestinian_authority
The Europe-based organization, which studies international issues, established this website to explain the impact of various organizations and governments on the politics of the Gaza Strip and West Bank. Visitors can find biographies of leaders of Hamas and the Palestinian Authority as well as articles on how history has unfolded in Gaza, leading to the Israel-Hamas War.

Israel Defense Forces
www.idf.il/en
The website for Israel's military provides updates on the war against Hamas, including videos filmed by IDF soldiers of the interiors of the Hamas tunnels in the Gaza Strip. By accessing the Live Feed link on the website, visitors can find minute-by-minute updates on IDF activities and the progress of Israeli forces in the war.

US Department of State: Israel-Hamas Conflict
www.state.gov/israel-hamas-conflict-latest-updates
The US Department of State established this website to provide updated information on the agency's efforts to engage Israel and Hamas in a ceasefire. Visitors can find numerous reports on the website outlining American diplomatic efforts, including meetings between US secretary of state Antony Blinken and world leaders.

INDEX

Note: Boldface page numbers indicate illustrations.

Abbas, Mahmoud, 15
Abu Anza, Rania, 55
Abusada, Mkhaimer, 29
Abu Saeid, Eman, 8
Abu Shaban, Eyad, 38
Al-Awda Hospital, 45–46
al-Lamdani family, 38
Alnajjar, Omar, 36
Arab countries, peace treaties with Israel, 14
Arab countries and Israel, 12, 14
Arafat, Yasir, **14**
Ardemagni, Eleonora, 55
Ashkelon, Hamas's attacks on, 20
Australia, 50

Bazelon, Emily, 10
Biden, Joe, 49, 51
Bitter, Kalina, 21
Brent, Aaron, 41–42

Clinton, Bill, **14**
Cohen, Gal, 22
Coleman, Adam B., 25
Conricus, Jonathan, 33
Council on Foreign Relations, 49–50

Dannatt, Richard, 47
deaths
  Hamas fighters, 31, 34
  Israelis
    after Hamas October 7 attack, 27
    during Hamas October 7 attack, 9, 20, 24–25
  IDF soldiers, 31
  Jews killed by Nazis, 11, 13, 27
  Palestinians in Gaza, 6, 38, **39**, 55
Deir al-Balah, 35
Dekel-Chen, Avital, 7–8
Dekel-Chen, Jonathan, 9
Dekel-Chen, Sagui, 6, 7–8, **7**, 9
Diller, Yoni, 20
Dreyfus, Alfred, 13

Eaton, Jason, 50
Egypt
  administration of Gaza by, 12–13
  Hamas and, 31–32
  humanitarian aid for Gaza and, 53
  peace treaty with Israel (1979), 14
  refusal to allow Gazan refugees into, 40
El-Nounou, Taher, 19

Finer, Jonathan, 51

food
  hidden in tunnels by Hamas for fighters only, 44
  supplies of
    to Gaza allowed to enter, 53–54, **54**
    to Gaza cut off, 34–36, 41–42, **43**
France, 50
Friedman, Thomas L., 6, 18
"From the river to the sea, Palestine will be free," **17**, 18
fuel
  hidden in tunnels by Hamas for fighters only, 44
  supplies of, to Gaza cut off, 34–36, 41–42

Galaria, Irfan, 44–45
Gallant, Yoav, 35
Gaza
  basic facts about, 13
  borders of, **12**
  conditions in, before war, 17, 18, 41
  deaths in, 6, 38, **39**, 55
  Egyptian administration of, 12–13
  food and fuel supplies cut off by IDF, 34–36, 41–42, **43**
  humanitarian aid for, 53–54, **54**
  Israeli hostages held in tunnels, 34
  Jewish settlements in, 16
  missile attacks on, 28, 39–40
  Oslo Accord and, 15–16
  refugees and Egypt, 40
  residents displaced by fighting, 36, 41
  Six-Day War and, 13–14
  unemployment in, 17
  water in, 42
  See also specific cities
Gaza City
  Hamas tunnels under buildings and streets of, 30–31
  Israeli missile attacks on, 8
  deaths from, 38, **39**
  destruction from, 29
  warnings to residents before, 28
Germany, 50
Gilad, Amos, 51
Gindi, Joe, 50
Great Britain, 11, 50

Hagari, Daniel
  on battles in tunnels, 34
  on Hamas rockets fired on Israel, 27
  on weapons stored in tunnels, 33
Haim, Yotam, 33
Hamad, Ghazi, 25–26, **26**

Hamas (Islamic Resistance Movement)
  attacks on Israel after October 7, 2023, 26–27, 48
  Egypt and, 31–32
  fighters
    deaths of, 31, 34
    estimated number of, 34, 44
    rapes committed by, 25
    street battles with IDF, 31, **32**
  foreign governments aiding, 50–51
  leadership of, 55
  Netanyahu and negotiations with, 51
  obliteration of, as aim of Netanyahu, 27, 28
  obliteration of Israel as goal of, 10, **17**, 18
  tunnels under Gaza City's buildings and streets described, 30–31
    food hidden in, for fighters only, 44
    weapons made and stored in, 32–33
    weapons seized by IDF, 33
  See also hostages taken by Hamas; October 7, 2023, attacks on Israel by Hamas
Hammash, Yousef, 42
Hamouda, Manal, 37–38
Hamouda, Tariq, 37–38
Harakat al-Muqawama al-Islamiya. *See* Hamas (Islamic Resistance Movement)
Harding, Emily, 22
Hawajri, Johan al-, 41
Herzl, Theodor, 13
Holocaust, 11, 13, 27
hostages taken by Hamas, 25
  held in tunnels under Khan Younis, 34
  from Kibbutz Nir Oz, 9
  killed by IDF, 33
  release of
    during ceasefire in exchange for militants, 48
    as goal of Netanyahu, 28
  at Supernova music festival, 20, **21**
  treatment by Hamas of, 48
Houthis, 55
Human Rights Watch, 53

Integrated Food Security Phase Classification, 41
international response, 47, 49
Iran, 51
Iron Dome defense system, 26–27, 48
Islamic Resistance Movement. *See* Hamas (Islamic Resistance Movement)

Israel
  borders of, 12, **12**
  Hamas and
    attacks on, after October 7, 2023, 26–27, 48
    obliteration of Israel as goal of, 10, **17**, 18
    rockets fired by, 27
  Likud government
    opposition to current actions by, 51–53, **52**
    politics and, 16
    settlements in Gaza, 16
    settlements in West Bank, 16–17
  Oslo Accord and, 15–16
  peace treaties with Arab countries, 14
  as refuge from future Holocaust, 27
  Supernova music festival in, 19–20, **21**, 25
  terrorist attacks against, 15
  UN mandate establishing and Arab attacks on, 10–11, 12
  US and, 49–50
  See also October 7, 2023, attacks on Israel by Hamas
Israel Defense Forces (IDF)
  attack on Rafah by, 55
  casualties, 31
  ceasefire (November 24, 2023), 48
  food and fuel supplies to Gaza cut off by, 34–36, 41–42, **43**
  Hamas leadership targeted by, 55
  Hamas's weapons seized by, 33
  humanitarian aid for Gaza and, 53
  Iron Dome defense system, 26–27, 48
  missile attacks on Gaza, 8
    deaths from, 38, **39**
    destruction from, 29, **35**, 39–40
    warnings to residents before, 28
  psychological effect of combat on, 33
  reserves, 24
  service in, 11
  street battles with Hamas, 31, **32**

Jabalia, 45–46
Jamal, Mahmoud, 29
Jerusalem, Hamas's attacks on, 21
Jordan, 12–13, 14

Khan Younis
  destruction in, **35**
  hospital in, 44–45
  Israeli hostages held in tunnels under, 34
kibbutzim
  basic facts about, 6–7
  Kibbutz Be'eri, 22–24, **23**
  Kibbutz Nir Oz, 6, 7–8, 9

safe rooms in, 7–8, 24
security teams, 23
Klemenson, Elhanan, 24
Klemenson, Menachem, 24

Lamdani, Dima al-, 38
Lebanon, 55
Likud Party, 15, 16, 17

MedGlobal, 44
medical care, 43–46, **45**, 54
Mossad, 22, 30

Nakba, 10, 13
Naor, Tomer, 16–17
negotiations, **49**, 51
Netanyahu, Benjamin, **29**
  American opposition to current actions by government of, 51–52, **52**
  Biden and, 49
  destruction of Hamas as aim of, 27, 28, 36
  Likud Party and, 16
  negotiations with Hamas and, 51
  Palestinian Authority and, 17
  two-state solution and, 17
New York Times, 44

October 7, 2023, attacks on Israel by Hamas
  background of, 18–19
  on cities, 20–22
  destruction of Israel as goal of, 25–26
  intelligence information about attacks, 22
  on Kibbutz Be'eri, 22–24, **23**
  on Kibbutz Nir Oz, 7–8
  planning of, 44
  at Supernova festival, 19–20, **21**
Ohana, Michael, 19
Olympics (1972), 15
Omar, Umm, 37
Oslo Accord (1993), **14**, 15–16
Ottoman Empire, 11

Palestinian Authority, 15–16, 17
Palestinian Liberation Organization (PLO), 14
Palestinians/Palestine
  history of area, 11
  Israel attacked by, 12
  as refugees, 13, 14
  UN mandate establishing, 12
psytrance music, 25

Qatar, 50–51, 53

Rabin, Yitzhak, **14**
Rabinovich, Itamar, 13
Rafah, 41, 55
Red Sea, shipping in, 55

safe rooms, 7–8, 24
Saleh, Basel, 55
Salha, Muhammad, 46
Saqallah family, 37–38, **39**

Sarandon, Susan, 53
Schem, Mia, 48
Scher, Corey, 40
Scholz, Olaf, 50
Schulzke, Marcus, 39
Schumer, Chuck, 51–52
self-defense, right of, 6
Shamriz, Alon, 33
Shoukry, Sameh, 40
Six-Day War (1967), 13–14
Solvy, Amit, 22–23

Talalka, Samer Al-, 33
Tel Aviv, Hamas's attacks on, 20–21
terrorism
  Hamas designated by US as organization of, 18
  hijacking of plane and Jews made hostages, 15
  by PLO against Israeli Olympic team (1972), 15
two-state solution, 16, 17

Ukrainian refugees, 40
United Nations (UN)
  mandate establishing Israel, 10–11, 12
  report on sexual assaults by Hamas, 25
United Nations Relief and Works Agency (UNRWA), 31
United States
  aid to Israel, 49–50
  hate speech and violence against Palestinians and Jews in, 50
  humanitarian aid for Gaza and, 53–54, **54**
  as Israel's closest ally, 49
  opposition to current actions by Netanyahu government, 51–52, **52**
  See also specific individuals

war, suffering of civilians during, 39
Washington Institute for Near East Policy, 32
Washington Square Park (New York City) demonstration, **52**, 52–53
water, 42, 44
West Bank
  basic facts about, 13
  borders of, **12**
  Jewish settlements in, 16–17
  Jordanian administration of, 12–13
  Oslo Accord and, 16
  Six-Day War and, 13–14
  unemployment in, 17
women raped by Hamas, 25
World Bank, 17
World Health Organization, 54
World War I, 11

Yaseen, Yousef Abdul Salam, 42
Yemen, 55

Zionism, 13, 50
Ziyad, Abu, 48